BASICS
TYPOGRAPHY
02

Using Type

Ethical: aware-
ness/
reflect-
ion/
debate

ava
academia

An AVA Book

Published by AVA Publishing SA
Rue des Fontenailles 16
Case Postale
1000 Lausanne 6
Switzerland
Tel: +41 786 005 109
Email: enquiries@avabooks.com

Distributed by Thames & Hudson (ex-North America)
181a High Holborn
London WC1V 7QX
United Kingdom
Tel: +44 20 7845 5000
Fax: +44 20 7845 5055
Email: sales@thameshudson.co.uk
www.thamesandhudson.com

Distributed in the USA & Canada by:
Ingram Publisher Services Inc.
1 Ingram Blvd.
La Vergne TN 37086
USA
Tel: +1 866 400 5351
Fax: +1 800 838 1149
Email: customer.service@ingrampublisherservices.com

English Language Support Office
AVA Publishing (UK) Ltd.
Tel: +44 1903 204 455
Email: enquiries@avabooks.com

© AVA Publishing SA 2010

ISBN 978-2-940411-55-9

Library of Congress Cataloging-in-Publication Data
Harkins, Michael.
Basics Typography 02: Using Type / Michael Harkins p. cm.
Includes bibliographical references and index.
ISBN: 9782940411559 (pbk.:alk.paper)
eISBN: 9782940447275
1.Graphic design (Typography).2.Graphic arts.3.Graphic arts--Study and teaching.
Z246 .H375 2011

10 9 8 7 6 5 4 3 2 1

Design by Create/Reject Ltd

Production by AVA Book Production Pte. Ltd., Singapore
Tel: +65 6334 8173
Fax: +65 6259 9830
Email: production@avabooks.com.sg

abc
def
ijk
lm
opqr

Table of contents

Introduction

Typography is a discipline within the wider context of graphic/communication design that produces results so ubiquitous and familiar to us that we are at times, and more often than not, oblivious to the existence of the subject itself. The wealth of knowledge related to typography, in addition to the rigorous practices and processes applied in order to create such work, are invisible for many, too. In most cases, this 'invisibility' is not achieved accidentally, but is more often purposefully generated by virtue of both the designer's skill and taste.

Good typographic design communicates appropriately in accordance with the demands placed upon it. The practice of typographic layout must balance the necessity of communication alongside aesthetic sensibilities. It must be informed by an understanding of convention and tradition, whilst demonstrating skill, judgment and taste in accordance with the zeitgeist. In short, the typographic designer can be seen as an arbiter of the visualization of language.

It has been said that good typography is invisible – a sentiment endorsed by Beatrice Warde in her famous lecture, 'The Crystal Goblet', given to the Society of Typographic Designers in London in 1932 – and this may be true to some extent. It is probably much fairer to say that good typography is more readily acceptable to us. Unfortunately, bad typography can also be invisible – not just for its intended recipients, but for those involved in producing it as well.

A lifelong student, teacher and practitioner, the German typographer, Jan Tschichold, once likened typography to 'clay in a potter's hand', claiming that '…there are no born masters of typography, but self-education may lead to mastery'. What Tschichold implied is that typography needs to be fundamentally understood in order to be practised; and practised in order to be understood.

This book aims to offer practical advice and guidance with regards to approaching the subject at an introductory to intermediate level, so that you can then put this new knowledge of using type directly to work. It is true to say that typography takes time to master, but once bitten by the typographic 'bug', you will find it very difficult to ignore it.

Typography acts as the designed visual embodiment of language; typographic layout, however, while facilitating the reading of language, can also be read in itself. It may be the content of a layout that is ultimately communicated, but the form of the typographic layout can be read too – in many cases, it is the shape and form of the layout that we 'read' first. The layout provides us with our first impressions, acting as the primary element in a hierarchy that can guide us along and through pages, that can express and convey meaning, and yet that can remain humble and perfunctory in its duty.

Whether designing a business card or a complete exhibition, a basic knowledge of the principles and practices related to typography is essential in order to produce useful and meaningful graphic design.

From choosing typefaces to setting text, designing grid systems to kerning headings, from understanding type as image to adjusting hyphenation and justification, this book will inform and assist you when making decisions about both the macro aspects of typographic layout and the detailing of typography at the micro level.

Along with constructive practical advice, examples of student and professional work contextualize and illustrate key points and themes found within the text, offering you the opportunity to develop a deep personal understanding of the subject.

In the fifteenth century, the earliest forms of typographic layout borrowed directly from strict doctrines of formal handwriting. The twentieth century progressed us from technologies barely improved upon since Gutenberg's invention of moveable type, through that of the avant-garde and asymmetric typography, delivering us into the digital realm. Now, in the twenty-first century, it will be you, the readers of this book, who will determine how the typographic landscape develops in the future.

Typography can best be described as the art
or practice of arranging letters and words.

But this description is perhaps too broad and
simplistic for us to make any *real* sense of what
typography is actually about. What kinds of letters
and words are we talking about? And produced
by what means?

Essentially, typography involves how letters and
words are arranged, how they are composed in
relation to each other, and the place they occupy
within a composition. Typography comes into play
when we choose fonts, decide how these are spaced,
what size they should appear at and how this affects
our reading of typographic arrangements. Sometimes,
the relationship between broad and specific aspects
of typographic practice can be referred to as macro
and micro typography. Whatever terminology we use
to describe this, we must firstly be able to identify
what exactly typography *is* and what it *is not*.

Seeing typography

In our daily lives, we are surrounded by so much typographic matter that we probably don't really notice that we are looking at things that have been *designed*; even though these things have often been designed in great detail. We take for granted that our favourite snack tells us about its nutritional content on the wrapper alongside its familiar branding.

It's not news to us that the book, magazine or newspaper we read on our daily journey to college or work was so easy to follow, not just because of its informative and entertaining content but also because it was well designed typographically, allowing us to read with ease and so keeping us engaged in that act of reading.

Opposite
It can sometimes take us a while to really 'see' typography; it is something we need to take time to appreciate. However, typography can be so obvious that we barely notice it at all. This optician, it would appear, has some very short-sighted clients.

Right
We sometimes see beautiful examples of what we think of as typography in the street around us. But is it really type?

'There is nothing simple or dull in achieving the transparent page. Vulgar ostentation is twice as easy as discipline. When you realize that ugly typography never effaces itself, you will be able to capture beauty as the wise men capture happiness by aiming at something else. The 'stunt typographer' learns the fickleness of rich men who hate to read. Not for them are long breaths held over serif and kern, they will not appreciate your splitting of hair-spaces. Nobody (save the other craftsmen) will appreciate half your skill. But you may spend endless years of happy experiment in devising that crystalline goblet which is worthy to hold the vintage of the human mind.'

Beatrice Warde Excerpt from *The Crystal Goblet, or Printing Should Be Invisible* (1956)
First addressed to the British Typographers' Guild (1932)

Typography in daily life

Imagine removing all the typography
from the local high street. Some might
argue that this would be a good thing,
but how would we find our way to the
local library, swimming pool or public
conveniences? It would probably be
quite inconvenient! Think a bit further.
How would we navigate the Internet?
How would we know how much of
our medication to take and at which
times? How long should the pizza take
to cook? We can't say that these things
would be impossible to do without the
existence of typography, but we can
say that typography has become such
an intrinsic part of daily life that we
would undoubtedly lead very different
lives without it.

Although typography may pervade
almost every aspect of our lives,
identifying what it is can sometimes
be a different matter. It can be a
little like listening to music. You may
know that you are listening to a tune
or a song, for instance – that's pretty
obvious isn't it? But do you know what
style of music it is? Which instruments
are being played? What timing the
music is set to and in which key it is
played? Recognizing typography is
very similar in many ways. Awareness
of what we are looking at (or listening
to in the case of music) is part of the
key to understanding the subject.

The nature of typography

One of the main things that it is helpful to distinguish if we are looking at various kinds of letterform is: are they all considered to be typography?

The answer is definitely: no!

The invention of moveable metal type is generally attributed to Johannes Gutenberg of Mainz, Germany in the mid-fifteenth century. Printing from moveable metal types meant that once a text had been printed, the arrangement of the types could be dismantled and then re-composed. This innovation, along with the means to print from a mechanical press, not only allowed for the production of multiple copies of texts but also made it far easier, much quicker and less expensive than producing the same texts as handwritten manuscript, as would have been the case prior to Gutenberg's invention.

The quality of the technology employed to allow for the interchangeability and potential to replicate letterforms becomes important when defining typography as something distinctly different to other methods of producing letterforms. Although modern technologies have changed dramatically since Gutenberg's time, mostly in the second half of the twentieth century, in many ways the essential nature of typography has changed very little.

Johannes Gutenberg (1398–1468)

Johannes Gutenberg (also known as Johannes Gensfleisch zur Laden zum Gutenberg) is credited as the German inventor of moveable metal type in conjunction with the creation of the printing press.

The first book of significance printed was the 42-line Gutenberg Bible, known as the Mazarin Bible, which is believed to have been printed around 1455.

Gutenberg devoted most of his adult life to developing his invention. Funds were raised from a wealthy moneylender and patrician, Johann Fust (1400–1466), allowing Gutenberg to continue with his work.

However, Fust eventually foreclosed on Gutenberg, taking control of his types, press and half of the printing business. Together with his son-in-law, Peter Schöffer, Fust became successful in printing and publishing bibles. Gutenberg, however, apart from receiving a small stipend in recognition of his achievements, died almost penniless in 1468.

What typography is

So how *is* typography defined precisely? We have so far described it as the art or craft of arranging letters and words. This is a very simplistic view and although it is in part correct, it is not wholly so. Typography also allows for the arrangement of letters and words (along with other visual matter) to be reassembled and replicated as few or as many times as is necessitated by the demands of what is to be communicated (the content).

Typography is bound by the constraints of the medium or technology (print, the Internet, and so on) through which it is to be disseminated. As well as being creative in terms of an art or craft, typography is a technical subject which demands certain standardizations and considerations of established methodologies and practices.

We could claim that early western typography (the invention of which, as we have already discovered, is generally attributed to Johannes Gutenberg) constitutes the mechanization of formal handwriting. This may not fit with current views on typography, but echoes of Gutenberg's and his immediate successors' achievements still clearly resonate today.

Typography uses signs (letters) to represent spoken and written language. There are elements of language that typography has no signs to represent (such as tone of voice, for example). There are also other 'typographic' signs (such as symbols) that have no utterance in language. Letters are signs that represent sound but as signs they have no meaning, just as the individual sounds (phonemes) have no meaning. Only when arranged together do they form words; and words are in turn signs (or labels) used to describe our environment, experiences and concepts.

Typography is concerned with both the creation of typeface and their arrangement to convey a message. It surrounds us in daily lives, enabling, guiding and directing us through the physical space. It differs according to time and Typography is... physical space. It differs according to time and place and can play many roles within its use. Overall, it is a form of art that moves and adapts with time.

Opposite
An exercise that explores students' personal definitions and understanding of typography at an early stage.

Right
Cartlidge Levene's in-house signage for the British newspaper, *The Guardian*, combines clarity and conspicuousness. It is both playful and sensitive in its application and use of materials.

Typography systematically visualizes language intended for readings by specific audiences. Whether designing a book of poetry or a poster for a museum, typography's job is to allow for the reading of language (as text) and to thus communicate information. Challenges as to how readers engage with typography and the act of reading have surfaced from time to time in the history of typographic practice, and interesting and curious work has emerged from this. However, the main purpose of typography is to enhance the act of reading texts, not to hinder it. It is also important for typography to act appropriately. Both the content of and the context for which a text is intended must form important considerations for the designer.

Typography can be engaged with at different levels. There is the holistic view: this comprises looking at the page, layout, composition, number of columns and interaction of text and images. And there is the detailed view: the choice of type, sizes, letter-spacing, word-spacing, line length, line-spacing, use of ligatures, small caps, drop caps and so on.

These two levels of engagement are sometimes referred to as 'macro' and 'micro' typography respectively. One is often neglected in favour of the other. Some designers see the macro view as 'creative' typography or graphic design. It is safe to say, however, that spending time understanding the finer 'details' of typography can only lead to enhance whatever ability the designer brings to the subject in a general design context.

Typographically speaking

If asked to design a brochure for a conference on the future of architecture, we wouldn't expect to see 'antique' or novelty fonts being used. Similarly, we wouldn't expect to see something so 'ultra modern' that it looks clichéd or resembles a pastiche of past visions of the future. We would need some awareness of the expectations of our audience and the typography would need to reflect these too. That's not to say that typography should not be fun and creative.

Typographically speaking, however, your design shouldn't turn up to the party in a chicken suit when the invitation is for black tie only!

Beatrice Warde observed that good typography should be like drinking wine from a crystal goblet. We should be allowed to concentrate on the wine and not be distracted by the vessel that carries it. This may similarly hold true, for instance, when we are reading a novel. We want to get into the narrative, get to know the characters and the plot. We're not necessarily interested or even aware of the type and typography involved in rendering this information.

However, we probably can't say that Warde's statement would ring true for all typography. If we are at a busy airport, for example, we do want to be aware of the typography around us, as we will want to find out how we get to where we need to.

Above
This student experiment playfully explores an understanding of type and typography through the physical printing of individual wooden types and their typographic arrangement. This allows for multiple readings of words and the connection to the printed word as expressive image.

We will want that typography to be clear too; but most importantly, we will need to notice it, although not in a way that detracts from what it is designed to be telling us.

Whether we follow Warde's example or not when we are designing typographic work, we do read before we read. That may sound odd, but we do this all the time without necessarily being aware of it. The layout, composition, use of colour, selection of typefaces, size of type, width of columns and so on within a design all combine to send out signals that we read as a whole before getting down to the job of reading the content.

Our favourite newspaper or magazine looks a certain way and has an identity of its own. So too do things like signage systems, information design and websites. No matter how creative or how neutral typography aims to be, it is impossible for it to *not* send out these design signals. It does take practice to develop control of this as a designer. Some people may also argue that you need to develop 'taste' too.

Taste, however, is a very subjective area. Being typographically 'aware' may be another way to think about this – adopting diverse (and appropriate) ways of thinking towards different problems. Like any other specialism, typography will take time to master.

Obviously, typography can be practised by producing and designing type matter, but practise can also come in the form of finding good exemplars, then making observations and asking questions of them. What typeface is being used? How many words appear within the column width? What size of type and leading might be used? Is there a grid system?

Finding the answers to such questions is where you need to put some effort in – consult type specimen books or online resources, measure text widths and print out text at various sizes, before comparing this to what you found originally. It is very important to develop your own working understanding of the subject. Typography requires active participation, even in the apparently simple act of reading.

'Typography has one plain duty before it and that is to convey information in writing. No argument or consideration can absolve typography from this duty. A printed work which cannot be read becomes a product without promise.'

Emil Ruder
Typographie (1967)

What typography isn't

So far, we have been describing typography in general terms, have noted that there are different levels of engagement with the subject and have discovered that our view of what typography *is* may develop over time as we engage further with the subject. In order to make clear our understanding of what typography *is*, it is also important to determine what typography *isn't*. To do this, we need to first clearly distinguish typography from other closely related subjects, crafts and activities.

Students beginning to study typography often have difficulty making distinctions between lettering and typography, particularly when that lettering is used within a graphic design context. This could be a highly stylized product name on a piece of packaging supported by typographic matter. In fact, it's not such an easy job for even seasoned graphic designers to make such distinctions sometimes!

Typography *isn't* lots of seemingly closely related subjects.

Typography *isn't*… handwriting.

Typography *isn't*… lettering.

Typography *isn't*… carving letters into stone or wood by hand.

Typography *isn't*… signwriting.

Typography *isn't*… graffiti.

Typography *isn't*… making letters from rubber bands.

Typography *isn't*…

That is not to say, however, that the letterforms produced by these other means cannot be made into type, which in turn could then become typography. Typography does not involve producing letters uniquely and individually each time by hand (or tool). However, there are fonts that allow letters to appear differently each time, both randomly and contextually. Indeed, Johannes Gutenberg's original Textura type contained alternative and contextual versions of letters that helped the setting of the type appear closer to the handwriting that he strove to emulate.

Opposite
Although fashioned in similar styles, the beautiful pen work (above) and stone carving (below) are not examples of typography. Both were made circa 1840 and draw on the earlier fashion for copperplate engraving. However, the influence of these crafts on the designing of type is clear.

Typography allows for the systematic replication of letters, words, sentences and paragraphs. So where does that leave stencils, rubber stamps, pressing letters into clay, potato printing even? These can be rearranged, replicated and produced in multiples too, can't they?

Making any definitive description of a subject is inevitably a difficult task because there will always be areas where subject boundaries, thinking and technologies develop and merge. This is why it is important to develop a personal view of typography based on your own knowledge and experience; as well as also being open to that view changing and developing as you gain further experience and knowledge.

Once you have the bug, typography isn't easy to ignore. You will find yourself looking at the spacing between letters (kerning) on newspaper headlines, you will become infuriated by inch marks that have been used instead of apostrophes, default and ubiquitous typefaces will have you pleading for strength – but you will delight at correctly considered leading (line-spacing)! As you develop your typographic sensibilities, you will notice things that many other people simply take for granted.

Typography *isn't*… something you learn overnight. Don't worry – no-one will expect you to either.

Looking at type

Whether we realize it or not, our everyday lives are saturated with typographic design. From the moment we pick up a cereal packet in the morning for our breakfast, to reading our favourite book last thing at night, we are looking at things that have been designed (although not always *well-designed*). We are oblivious to most forms of typographic design – we read the information or content that the design carries, rather than studying the designed artefacts as things in themselves. This is sometimes how the designer of that product or type would like us to perceive the design.

Task 1

Document one day of your life acting as an observer of typographic design, producing a comprehensive diary of the typographic experience of your day from first thing in the morning to last thing at night.

Keep this diary within a research folder or sketchbook. You should be prepared to use photography, photocopying and other means where necessary to evidence what you find, as well as collecting first-hand examples of typographic design.

Use annotation to reflect on what you have collected and documented. Your annotations should help you to consider what kind of design it is that you are recording.

For example, a cereal packet may have some large obvious lettering / typographic device on the front face of the box, but there will also be typography in the form of information design within a 'Nutritional Information' table on the packaging. So are you looking at promotional design/ branding or information design? Or are you looking at typography? Is it lettering?

Choose two examples of design that you have collected that you consider to have either good or bad qualities. Try to analyze these further in terms of their typography. Can you identify the typefaces being used? Does the typography communicate successfully? If so, *why*? If not, *why not*? Discuss your findings with others. Can they begin to make any distinctions between lettering and typography?

Terminology

Like all specialist subjects, typography has related terminology that must be learnt too. Learning the 'language' of typography not only helps develop greater personal understanding of the subject, but also allows you to communicate with peers in an appropriate and authoritative manner. There are words used to describe typography that as a novice you will have never heard before.

There are also familiar words used that take on completely new meanings when used in different contexts. You could find that your typography is full of orphans, widows and rivers if not resolved very well. You may also find that the typeface that you decided to use has a floppy ear, large beaks, stumpy legs and a protruding chin!

Many professions need specialist vocabularies to explain unique and specific attributes in relation to their practices. Historically, professional jargon has also helped to protect, separate and to give identity to such occupations – at times, the practice of using subject-specific language would partly and purposefully prevent these professions from being easily approached and understood by outsiders.

Typography is no exception. Much of the terminology used today has a long history associated with it. It can be argued that much of it makes no real logical sense today in terms of technology and practice. However, if the subject is to be understood, it is necessary to speak the same language as other practitioners of typography.

Typography is a discipline in itself. However, it is also a specialism or aspect embedded within other professions. Graphic designers, publishers, web developers, film-makers and games developers (to name but a few) all use typography within the context of their own subject at times. It is not always the case that a specialist typographer will be called upon to work with others in such fields, however; it is more likely that designers in other disciplines will produce their own typographic matter and with this a 'typo-language' that may at times differ from one discipline to the next.

Above
The first of the eight
issues of the seminal
*Octavo Journal of
Typography*, which
appeared from the
mid-1980s to the 1990s,
draws our attention to
how the great designers
of the past sought to
define their practice
through language.

It is not within the scope of this book to cover every nuance of the ways in which typography can be described, but to rather lay out some well-recognized and commonly accepted foundations for describing aspects of the subject, so that you can build upon these as your experience of typography grows. Again, this is something that will come with time, but it is also important to see this 'typo-language' as integral to typographic practice itself.

Terms such as 'kern', although historic, do not have exactly the same meaning when used in relation to digital type as opposed to the original lead. We use the words 'kern' and 'kerning' today to describe how the space between letters is decreased or increased. In relation to lead type, a kern is a part of a letter that overhangs its 'body' and thus encroaches on the 'body' space of a neighbouring character.

A ligature is different from a dipthong in that although these are both examples of conjoined characters, the combination of letters in the ligature does not directly change the pronunciation of the sound that the letters represent. Conversely, the dipthong does indicate a specific change in sound.

Opposite
This diagram introduces some useful terminology in relation to type and typography. An understanding of the language of type will also help you to clarify the concepts.

All typography implies tradition and conventions. Traditio derives from Latin trado, I hand over. Tradition means handing over, delivering up, legacy, education, guidance.

Jan Tschichold
The Importance of Tradition in Typography, Leipzig (1964)

Systems of measurement

Specific typographic language permeates all areas of the subject and measurement is not excluded. At some point when working with type, you will start measuring page sizes, margins and column widths. Generally, you will stick to what you know: inches, centimetres and millimetres. Type and typography, however, use additional units of measurement specific to the subject. The most common of these is the 'point' or 'pt'. This will be a fairly familiar term to most people who have used a personal computer, and if you have selected a type size in a word-processing or page layout program, you will no doubt have chosen the type size in points. One postscript point is equal to 0.353mm.

The point

The point is the smallest unit of typographic measurement. Its invention can be traced back to the work of French clergyman Sébastien Truchet and was derived from the 'Pied du Roi' – the French Royal Foot. French type-founder Pierre Simon Fournier, influenced by Truchet, defined a typographic point system in 1737. It was French printer François-Ambrose Didot who adapted the 'point system' (circa 1780), making it $\frac{1}{72}$ of an inch, which then became popular throughout continental Europe.

Due to early differences between the French inch and the British Imperial inch, Didot's point was larger than its British or American counterparts. This can all seem quite confusing when we look at it today. Now, however, the point system has been standardized for the personal computer, so a point in Paris is the same as a point in Mumbai. This is the 'PostScript point' or 'DTP point'. It is the measurement that appears as the default for type in most computer software programs.

Right
This composing stick would have been used to arrange individual lead types into lines of copy set to the measure in picas as can be seen on the gauge.
Here, 12 picas is equal to (approximately) two inches (50.8mm).

The pica

The pica is another unit specific to typography and is related to the point. There are 72 picas to one foot, just as there are 72 points to one inch. That means that there are 12 points in one pica and six picas to one inch.

The em or quod

The em or quod was a space unit in lead type equivalent to the size of the body of the associated type. Simply, if you used 12pt type, the size was given for the block (or body) of lead that the letterform appeared on. The em was relative to the height and width of the body for the upper-case M. The em unit is still used today and is still relative to the size of the type in use. Divisions of the em are given when adjusting letter-spacing in most software programs today. An en is half the width of an em.

Combining measurement

As mentioned earlier, there is much from the history of type and typography in terms of language (and measurement, for that matter) that is still current in modern usage. Of course, you can work and specify measurements in millimetres, for instance, and this would make sense; that is, until making conversions to and from point sizes, which is when things can become a little tricky.

It is fair to say that many designers will work using combinations of measurement systems for what suits them best or for what works best on a given project. It is not uncommon to see page sizes, for instance, specified in 'mm', 'cm' or inches (some designers still use picas, too), whilst type matter is specified in points (pt).

As will be discovered later (and with experience), even when making the most accurate specifications in typography, the eye will ultimately be the judge. In the end, typography deals with visual matter and no amount of measuring or applying mathematical principles will correct that which the eye detects as not fit for purpose.

Right
Previous to the computer, various forms of typographic rule were used to measure both setting widths and type line-depths.

Opposite
The basic unit of measurement in typography is still the point (pt), although other measurements can be used. This diagram shows incremental values from six to 72 points. You will notice how a corresponding type size appears smaller than the actual point size. To the right are respective em units relative to the body of the type.

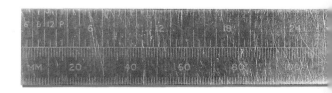

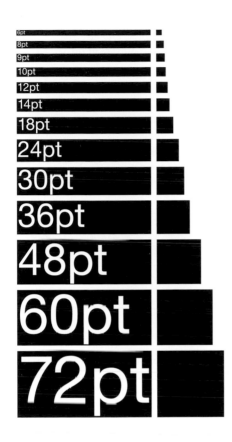

HOW TO
GET THERE

1966

Price 1/-

If you were planning to visit a major city – perhaps
for the first time – the chances are that you wouldn't
attempt the trip without some degree of planning.
You would probably have a reason for going to that
place, perhaps to see someone or something.
You would probably work out a route for getting there.
You would even build in some extra time to get there
in the event that you might be delayed on your journey.
It would make perfect sense to most people that such
an ordinary journey should be planned and that there
may be some unexpected events to deal with along
the way, so some sort of contingency plan may be
allowed for.

Similarly, typography needs to be planned. You need
to know what sort of journey it is you are taking. Is your
design intended for print or digital media? Have you
understood what has been asked of you in terms of
the brief that has been set? How will you arrive at your
design destination? This chapter looks at some of the
considerations you may need to make even before the
process of designing begins.

Content and context

It is a mistake to think that typography is an art, or worst still that it *is* art. It is true – and in this there is something of a paradox – that it is impossible to remove our personality from the act of designing. That is to say, that even when we try to be as objective as we possibly can in terms of design, something of our personality will always inevitably show through in that work. Design ultimately strives to produce solutions in answer to problems that have been set.

However, that is not always the same thing as problem-solving. Because design is subjective, there is always more than one answer to the problem set; so designers need to be aware of what exactly is being asked of them, how they work towards such design practice and what is ultimately informing their practice.

If a client asks a designer to produce some work, it is only right that the client should feel that they have been listened to, that it is their issues or problems that are being addressed and that they are not ignored at the expense of the designer forcing their own agenda on the project at hand.

Design can be opportunistic – it can seize upon a momentary observation, an accident or happening. It can also be meticulous, thorough and rigorous. However, it is *not* design if the designer chooses to make a personal statement above and beyond what is being asked of them.

Some of the best design finds its answers within the problems set. It connects form and communication – both functioning equally. It draws upon what needs to be communicated and delivers this appropriately to its intended audience.

COMING SOON: ARNHEM CENTRE & STORE FOR ART DESIGN FASHION

Left
Experimental Jetset's identity for the Dutch clothes store 'Coming Soon: Arnhem' (now renamed 'Arnhem: Coming Soon') interprets the store's modular, grid-like interior through the use of geometric form.

Audience

Another very important consideration to bear in mind is the intended audience or end user of the design. Who will read or see the work? Where will it be seen or be made available? What will it be used for?

Identifying your intended audience not only helps with how successfully your design will communicate, it will also help to give direction to the development of the design work itself. There are important considerations to make between the balance of content, context and form when designing. However, awareness of the audience or readership of the intended work should not be overlooked or underestimated.

Great design does not just communicate clearly but also effectively and efficiently. Knowing your audience, or more correctly, anticipating how your audience will perceive your work, may take some time to develop as a designer, but it is an aspect of design that should never be taken for granted either.

Certain audiences will have particular expectations; they will want to see things that conform to some visual orthodoxy that they have become familiar with over time. Others will want to be guided, challenged, thrilled or entertained. It is the job of the designer to know what kind of work to deliver in order to meet such expectations – not just for the client, but for the client's clients, too.

Above

In Phil Baines' design for Richard Grayson's 'The Golden Space City of God' exhibition at Matt's Gallery in London (2009), the juxtaposition of the formal text setting and playful display type reflect an audience who are open to challenging, visually sophisticated work.

Appropriateness

As designers, we are usually keen to develop our own understanding of our subject, and so we sometimes ask questions about why we should do things in certain ways. We may want to engage in producing work that pushes toward the cutting edge of the subject, even subverting the accepted or perceived wisdom of what has gone before. This is commendable and should be encouraged as such questioning can broadly help to develop the subject of design.

As designers, we must develop a good awareness of appropriateness, as it is one of the most important considerations to heed when planning a project. This is because if we think about how appropriate our work is, we need to consider many things in terms of the design, such as content, context, form, use, audience and self-authorship.

When we think about how appropriate our work is, we start to ask some very useful questions such as: what am I doing? Why am I doing it in this way? Who is it for? How might it be perceived or used?

Asking such questions of the work we produce helps us to begin to engage more critically with the subject of design. This is not just to understand design problems per se, but also to understand the way in which we approach such problems. Ultimately, we must ask the question: design for whom? And: how will that design be useful? Thinking about appropriateness doesn't mean that our work will be dry and boring. It does mean, however, that we can start to think about the work that we produce with both integrity and honesty.

Left
The typography on this vehicle certainly draws attention. Based on the chosen type, however, what kind of work would you expect this company to offer?

Above
Catherine Dixon's typography draws upon history and celebrates the relationship of the visible word to liturgical text.

Right
Here a tragedy has already occurred! The use of Comic Sans for such a serious notice appears inappropriate on many levels.

HELP PREVENT A TRAGEDY

If you see children or adults inside or attempting to enter this substation please call 08000 727282 or the local police immediately

SSE Power Distribution

Thinking ahead

It is often overlooked, especially in the early stages of learning how to design, or of becoming a designer, but knowledge or awareness of some of the technical considerations of production and process can help with conceptual development of the design work and the question of how a designer initially approaches this.

This section of the book highlights some aspects of production and process that you may find useful in informing your decision-making relative to your creative approach to design. Developing a sound working knowledge of methods, materials and processes of production is essential if a designer is to realize their conceptual work effectively. Indeed, knowledge of production and process can occasionally become the main impetus for creative work.

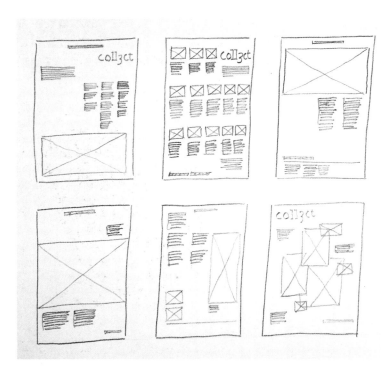

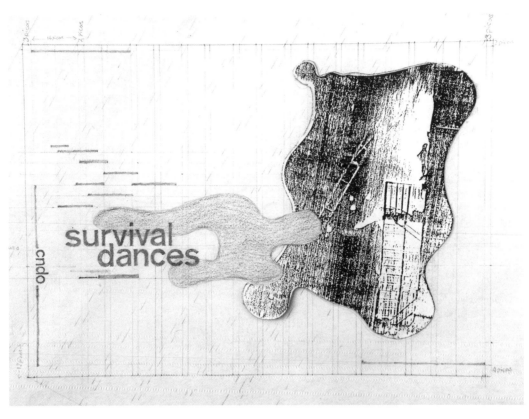

Opposite
At a very early stage, thumbnail sketches can help us to think about numerous elements of our design in relation to the concept.
Here, format and the underpinning grid for a design is implied, in addition to the overall layout.

Above and right
A precise and detailed sketch includes chosen format, measurement, custom-grid system and typeface.

Page plans

Page plans can start as a simple thumbnail sketch for a single page design or form a more ordered scheme that outlines the number of pages within a publication and the sequence in which these will be ordered. More often, it is the case that these will be combined in the form of a flatplan to give an overview of the work to be completed.

Thumbnail sketches can be very helpful in determining the composition of text and image elements within individual pages, the positioning of these in relation to margins, whether pages will have a symmetrical or asymmetric bias, and of how elements may be grouped together to give a feel for the general content and structure of each page. Producing thumbnails is a very useful exercise – these can be produced very quickly and can give clear guidance as to how the design will develop.

Flatplans not only give us an overview of the number and sequence of pages that we may be working with but also enable us to consider breaking down our work into manageable sections. They are especially useful when handling large numbers of pages. Whether you're designing a book, magazine, brochure or annual report, there is a good chance that you will need to consider things like sections or chapters. How will colour work across sections? Will you use several papers for different sections of the design?

Typography is as much about planning how things will work as it is about creating new or exciting work. Creating thumbnails and flatplans should become an essential aspect of efficient typographic practice. This not only helps us to handle the production of design, but (with planning) to forecast the way in which certain aspects of a large job will behave or appear prior to finalizing the work, too.

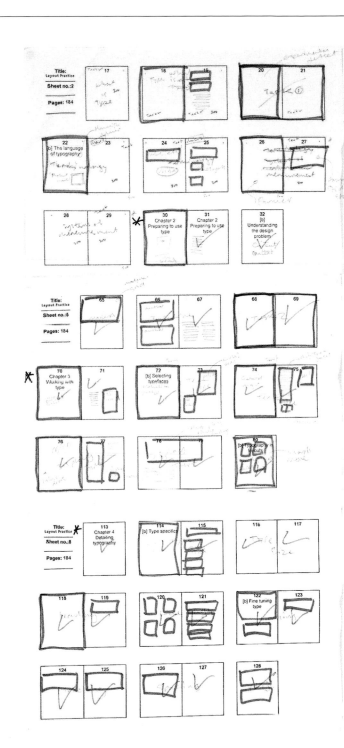

Right
Page plans or a flatplan are very useful when working with larger projects. Planning and workflow can be incorporated using a single plan. This helps to give a complete overview of the work.

Impositions

If thumbnails and flatplans help us to handle and organize the content and sequence of large volumes of typographic design, knowing something about imposition is very useful because this is how our work will appear in production when printed.

If our work is to be reproduced in large quantities, the chances are that work will be printed on a printing press rather than on our personal desktop printing devices.

Unlike the flatplan used for planning our design/production work, an imposition is how our final designed pages must appear in relation to each other on large single printed sheets so that they may be backed-up – that is, folded and gathered together once printed – to form the correctly ordered pagination.

Impositions normally consist of multiples of four pages, i.e. 4, 8, 16, 32, 64 and so on. This is of course determined by the size of the printed sheet in relation to the designed page. For example, if you were to design an A4 (210 × 297mm) brochure and the printer was using a sheet size of SRA2 (an over-sized A2 format for printing measuring 450 × 640mm that allows printers to apply registration marks, trim marks, colour bars and so on necessary for print production), the pages would appear with four printed on each side of the sheet. This would then be folded and trimmed to produce A4-sized pages. The pages would 'back' each other in the correct sequence.

It is very useful to know how your work will eventually be produced. This can open up further possibilities for refining your approach to design but will also open up creative possibilities in terms of considering formats, papers, inks, finishes and bindings. This knowledge will come with practice and experience, and through discussions with printers.

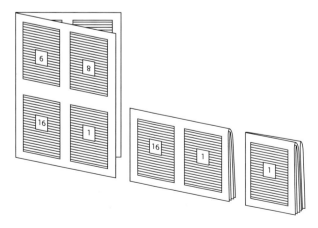

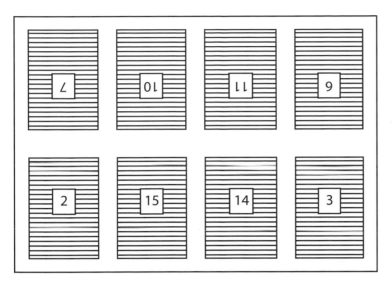

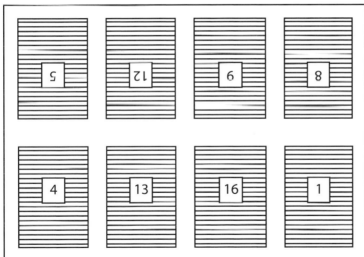

Left
An example of a
16-page (eight
pages on each side)
imposition, planned
as it will be printed
using offset litho.
A knowledge of printing
processes can help to
push your creative and
conceptual work too.

Opposite
The same imposition
folded down to form
a 16-page section.
Knowing how sections
print may help us when
making choices about
paper, ink colour and
so on.

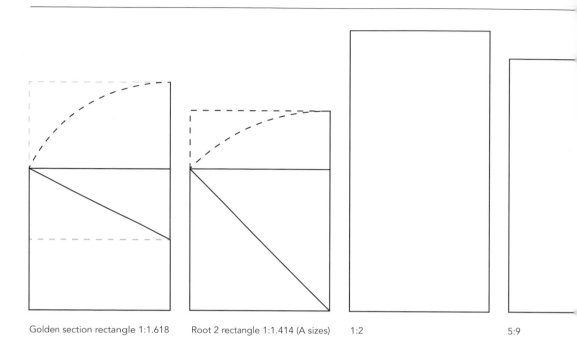

Golden section rectangle 1:1.618   Root 2 rectangle 1:1.414 (A sizes)   1:2   5:9

::

Selecting formats for work

There are many considerations to take into account when selecting formats for typographic design. Ultimately, page formats are determined by the size of the paper that the finished design will print upon. This may sound obvious, but it requires a little more investigation than you might at first expect!

How the work is to be printed will pose a certain amount of constraint on the sizes selected for design. It is within these print sizes that printed pages must be planned. From business cards to posters to books (and everything in between) it makes sense to know how the work will eventually be produced before selecting the appropriate format for design. This not only has a bearing on aesthetic considerations but may also have some impact on ethical or environmental concerns too, in terms of the amount of waste generated, for instance.

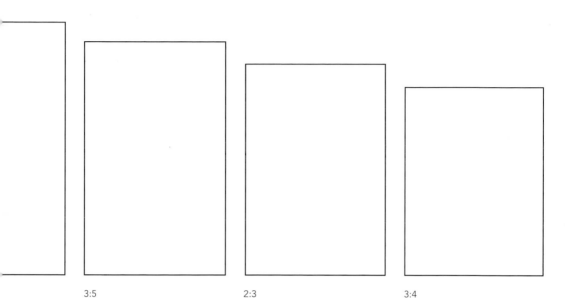

3:5 2:3 3:4

Above
Shown here are some
common proportions
useful for printed matter.
The Root 2 rectangle
proportion (A sizes) may
appear slightly static
in comparison to the
others, if we become
used to seeing it
too often.

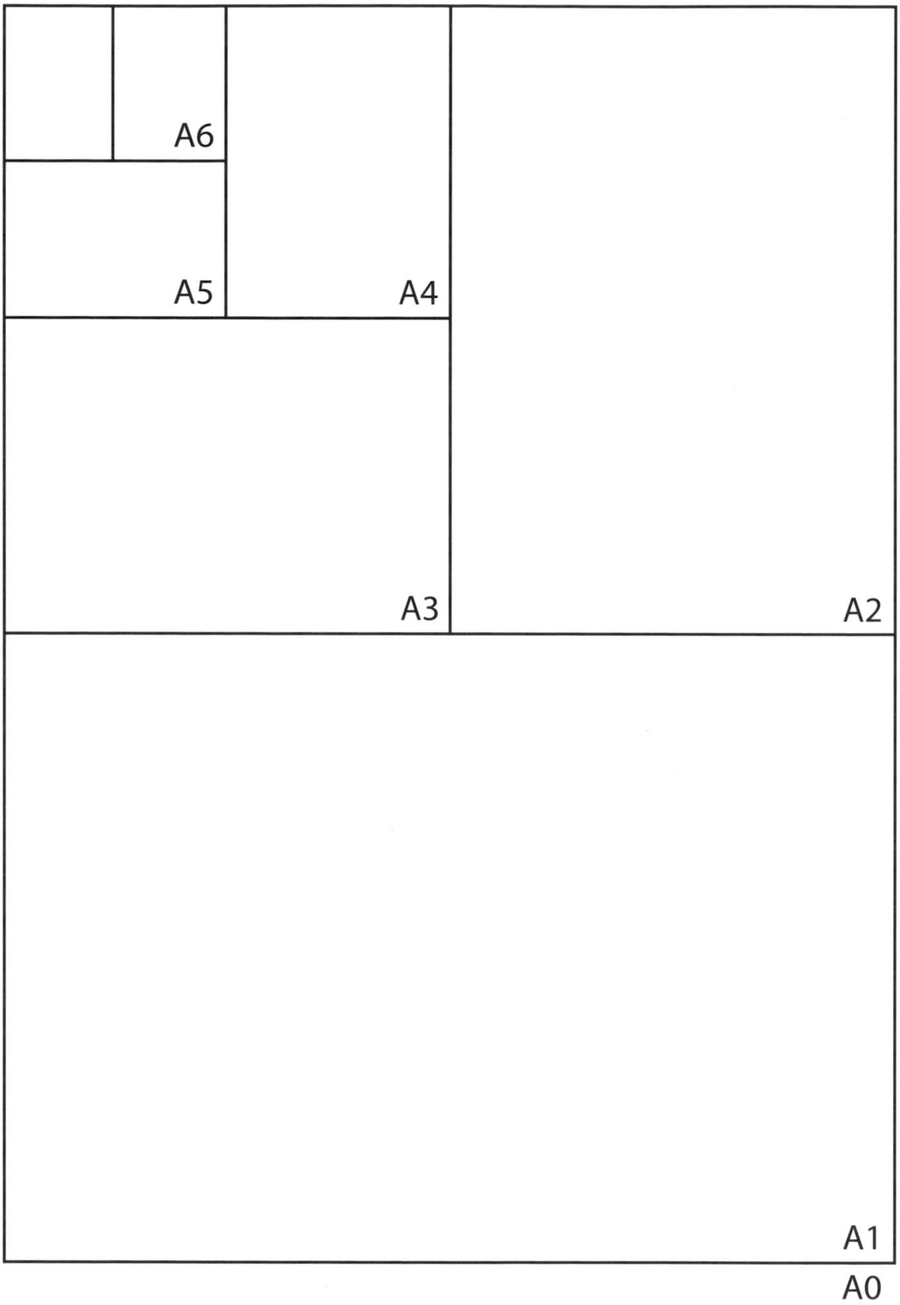

A6

A5

A4

A3

A2

A1

A0

Considerations of size

Choosing the correct size of format to work with is important, but so too is proportion. Sometimes, sizes will be selected for convenience or in conformity with expected standards. In Europe, for example, corporate stationery letterhead paper may conform to A4 (210 × 297 mm) size in most cases, which makes perfect sense since office and desktop printers are set to this default output size. Or, a book design may conform to a size that the publisher has predetermined because it fits within a given series.

The ISO standard paper sizes are used throughout the world with the exception of the system used by the USA and Canada, where many formats are regulated by American National Standards. If you are producing work for US or Canadian clients, be sure to check both the correct paper sizes and the relationship between the ratios of the sizes.

While the ISO system enjoys a uniform aspect ratio, the US system alternates between two ratios: 17/11=1.545 and 22/17=1.294; this means that you cannot reduce or magnify from one format to the next without leaving a vacant margin.

However, a great deal of design demands subtle consideration. Books that are to be held for reading rather than placed on a table need to be thought about in terms of the size and proportion of their pages, as well as the final number of pages that they will contain in order to ensure that the resulting product will be comfortable to use for the reader.

A poster may need to be of a sufficient size to be read from both far away and close up. More specific dimensions may need to be considered depending upon where the poster will appear. For example, if the poster is due to appear in bus shelters or on underground trains, these sites will require that the design work is produced to a given size. Other work may be far more arbitrary in its consideration.

Opposite
The proportions of the 'A' sizes allow for efficiency and regularity. Each time an 'A'-size sheet is folded in half, it creates a new 'A' size retaining the same ratio of proportion as before (1:1.414). The shortest length of the format is equal to half the longest length.

Production

The following pages briefly discuss some further aspects related to production that should be borne in mind when designing typographic work. Although in the early stages of learning to design you will no doubt give more attention to conceptual thinking and be focused on problem-solving, it is also really useful to think about how your design work may be produced or reproduced in the real world. This can also help you to think purposefully and creatively about the best achievable results possible.

Aside from the rare but valuable opportunities of working with wood and metal types in letterpress, most typographic work will eventually be produced on a computer.

Letterpress can be useful to us when learning about typography not because of any romantic or nostalgic associations that it may have, but simply because it means that we become involved in the whole process of designing through to printing. This makes the theoretical tangible. It gives us a clear insight of what happens to our single design, of how this needs to adapt if we introduce more than one colour and of how this in turn then translates at the printing stage of the process. It requires us to think about the size and type of paper that we might choose to print on and the effect that this will have on our design, as well as of how the work will be trimmed, folded and finished.

It therefore makes sense to develop your thinking about how design work produced on the computer might translate to print also. In the early stages of learning to design, most work will be printed to either personal or commercial laser or inkjet printers. This is of course to be expected. However, if a design is to be reproduced in large quantities, then commercial digital, off-set litho or gravure printing perhaps need to be considered too.

Above
The physical size of
type, arrangement and
colour separation are
a few of the elements
we are forced to
consider when working
in letterpress. Practical
considerations that
focus on process are
very valuable.

Dummies and mock-ups

Typographers and graphic designers are much like designers in other fields. When we start designing a piece of work, we may soon produce a mock-up or dummy of that work. This can appear to all intents and purposes as a very convincing piece of design. Architects may produce sketches and drawings to begin with – much as we do. They may produce models or maquettes of their designs – much as we do. However, architects would not normally build life-size models of the buildings that they design, clad with the correct facing stone and with functioning details such as windows and doors.

Yet, as typographers and graphic designers, that's almost exactly what we do when we produce good quality mock-ups of our work. We may be using the correct text, and the appropriate font and images. We may have specified the exact colours for the design scheme. But because we work so closely with material that could convincingly pass for the finished article, we sometimes neglect to ask further reaching questions of it.

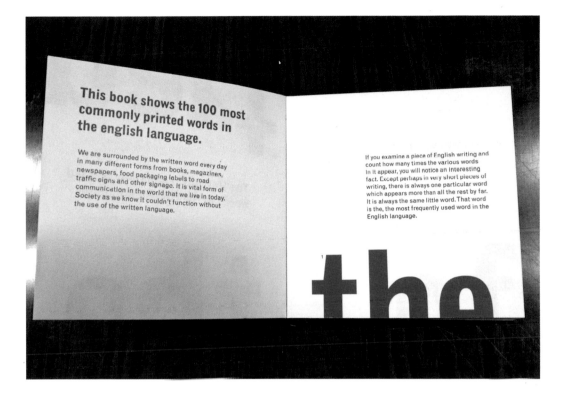

Within the image:

This book shows the 100 most commonly printed words in the english language.

We are surrounded by the written word every day in many different forms from books, magazines, newspapers, food packaging labels to road traffic signs and other signage. It is vital form of communication in the world that we live in today. Society as we know it couldn't function without the use of the written language.

If you examine a piece of English writing and count how many times the various words in it appear, you will notice an interesting fact. Except perhaps in very short pieces of writing, there is always one particular word which appears more than all the rest by far. It is always the same little word. That word is the, the most frequently used word in the English language.

the

Opposite
A high level of attention can be seen in this successful ISTD student workbook dummy.

Above
The level of professionalism is continued throughout in the student workbook. Due consideration was given to paper, boards, printing processes, format and binding, as well as to concept and design.

What printing process will be needed to produce this work? What types of inks will be used? How will the folding or binding be specified? What materials will be available for production?

These represent only a few questions that we might ask of the design, but they shouldn't come as a surprise to students of graphic design and typography. After all, you would expect an architect to know something about construction, materials, building regulations, stresses and loads, wouldn't you?

Paper

The success of a typographic design benefits from and in many cases can largely depend on the considered selection of substrates. The term 'substrate' is used to refer to any material that is used for printing on. In the majority of cases, this will be paper or board (card). If we work directly on a computer, the chances are that we will print our work onto bright white laser and inkjet papers. This may help to show the printer's toners at their best performance, but it is unlikely to do much for the design produced in terms of its subtle qualities or tactile nature.

It can be argued that the selection of a good, or even of the correct, paper can make or break the success of a design. But it is not just the colour or the tactile qualities of the paper that we need to consider – we need to think about the weight too. The weight of paper is often specified in grams per square metre (gms) or in microns (particularly boards). This can also have an effect on the designed work.

Papers are commonly referred to as uncoated and coated stock. Coated paper is usually coated with an agent such as china clay to give a smooth, flat surface. This can help to improve the opacity of the paper, colour absorption and the lustre or appearance of the printed image. Coated papers can come in a range of finishes from flat matt to high gloss.

Uncoated papers may give a natural feel to the printed work, and there is likely to be less glare from it, which can be useful when considering things like the contrast between typographic matter and the page. Many books set for continuous reading (for example, novels) use uncoated papers, which are usually off-white or cream in colour. The effect is gentler on the eye than 'high' or bright white paper and usually makes for a more comfortable read. It is worthwhile researching paper suppliers and manufacturers. Building a library of paper samples is important for any aspiring typographic designer.

Left
A special translucent paper was sourced for this book that becomes a poster. Reading is 2D across the surface and 3D through the pages as they unfold. The paper is thus critical to the success of the design.

Opposite
Collecting a library of paper and board samples is important. These details can often be seen as an afterthought but are also important considerations to take into account.

Inks

Most of the devices we print to will be based on laser printer or inkjet printer technology. This is true of commercial digital printing too. There are of course many benefits to this; it lets us produce proofs of work rapidly and is relatively inexpensive when compared to other forms of printing. However, when we design a piece of work for print and that work is to be reproduced in large numbers (for example, 5oo+), it is likely that this will be printed via offset lithography.

When we print to a laser or inkjet printer, the files we send to print are processed so that we get a composite result in terms of any colour that we have used in our design. That is to say, software between the program we use and that installed on the printer interprets the colours we specify to give us the best result.

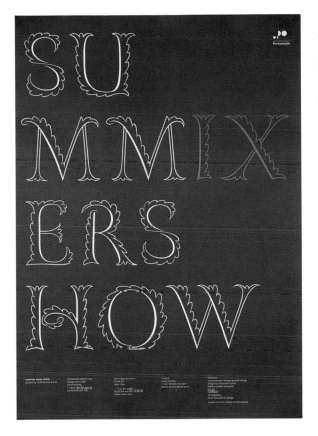

When designing for print, the types of colours used are very important. Colours for print should be specified as cyan, magenta, yellow and black (or the key colour) – otherwise known as CMYK. Alternatively, 'spot', 'solid' or 'special' colours should be specified, such as those of the Pantone® Matching System or 'PMS colours'. This is because work printed by offset litho must be 'colour separated' and each colour is then printed in sequence. If you have colour within your design, this will be made up from percentages of CMYK overprinted in combination, unless you are using solid or single colours.

Spot colours are individual inks that give a specific colour related to proprietary matching systems. These colours may often be difficult to achieve using the 'four-colour process' of CMYK due to the specific pigments that they are made from. However, a design may actually be enhanced by the use of a limited colour palette. A 'two-colour' design that uses one spot colour and black, for example, can appear very effective; it will also reduce costs in terms of litho printing, as fewer separated printing plates will ultimately be needed.

Opposite
Colour, inks and production are important factors to consider when thinking about how design is 'reproduced'.

Above
Two Pantone Hexachrome® inks are used in this poster to achieve a brighter result.

Print finishing

When our design work is professionally printed, we may also want to consider that there are options open to us that are impossible to simulate using our desktop printers. This goes beyond the effects achieved using well-selected paper and correctly specified inks. This may include specifying metallic inks, overprinting, laminations, varnishes and foil blocking. To this we can add folding, creasing, embossing and die-cutting, to name just a few other processes.

It is not possible to acquire knowledge of all these additional processes when starting out as a designer; however, it is useful to know what exists beyond that which can be produced from desktop printing devices. Contact with a reputable local printing firm can be very useful as you are likely to gain many insights from them as to what is possible from a professional perspective.

As with all design considerations, applying special finishes to a job must be carefully considered. There is no use in applying all the 'bells and whistles' to a job if the design itself is poor. This won't have the effect of compensating for what has been ill-considered – it is more likely to draw attention to the fact. However, a considered and confident selection of print finishes can add something special to a design that would be impossible to achieve in any other way.

Above
The packaging shown
here forms part of Made
Thought's identity for
The Mill. The quality of
the materials and print
finishing is paramount to
the effectiveness of the
visual identity.

Binding

Binding is the process of gathering and fastening loose printed sheets (signatures) in the correct order to form a single publication. This often includes an outer cover to protect the pages within.

There are several standard forms of binding and many unique and special forms are also possible. Again, this is an important consideration for the typographic designer when producing multi-page designs.

Standard binding includes the following:

Saddle-stitching

This is a way of basically creating 'stapled' publications or books of up to around 80 pages maximum. There is no spine for a title or other information about the book.

Perfect binding

Pages are gathered into the correct order to form a block. Glue is applied to the spine edge of the block and then a cover (usually made of paper or light card) is attached to the glued edge. This is then trimmed flush at the top, bottom and fore-edge when dry. Magazines, brochures and paperbacks may be perfect bound.

Case binding

This can be readily seen in hardback books. Signatures are gathered and sewn together for strength. The block of pages is trimmed on three sides and the 'end papers' are glued onto the inside front and back of a constructed hardback case. Perfect-bound blocks can also be bound in hard cases reducing the cost of sewing the printed signatures together; these are considered less durable, however.

Other standard forms of binding include wire or spiral binding, comb binding, side-stitching, lay-flat binding, tape binding, post binding and velo binding. This gives some indication of the range of processes available to the designer and requires careful attention and research in relation to the designed matter.

Above
Shown here are some
examples of binding.
From top: coptic / kettle
stitch; perfect binding
(example: soft cover);
comb binding; saddle-
stitch (or stapled);
and case binding
(example: hardback).

Order and structure

Graphic designers and typographers often use grids as an aid to help with organizing text and image matter in relation to the page. Grids can help to give order, structure and clarity to a design. They can help create hierarchy, accuracy and identity also. Not all typographic design will require the use of a grid and many successful designs, and designers, do not employ them in their work. However, using a grid system in typographic design work in its simplest form offers a guide to proportion and accuracy – a safety net. For the most capable designers, grids can offer a methodological framework for creativity in relation to design.

So what is a grid? In most cases, a grid is simply a set of drawn lines that mark out where text and image matter may appear on a page. This can include margins, columns and gutters (the space between columns). Grids can mark out a single text area, as found in some book designs, for example. They can also be multi-column or modular grid systems that may be used in newspaper or magazine design. The complexity of a grid can vary depending on its intended use. For the reader or viewer of the finished design, the grid remains invisible, like much of the work of typographic practice.

A grid may be measured, exact and mathematical. As with other aspects of typographic design, however, the eye is the ultimate judge as to whether something works visually or not. A grid is used to aid and guide design – and should not become a straightjacket or imposing template. Sometimes, the grid will need to be broken or adjusted so that the design will work properly. This is to be expected. A grid should allow a design to flourish if handled correctly. A grid should never become a framework for monotony.

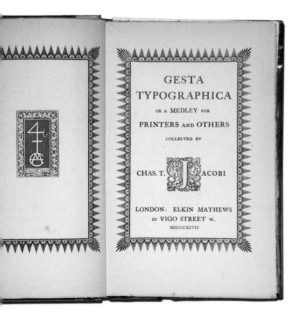

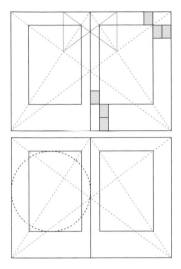

Jan Tschichold's canons appear similar to another traditional established system of proportion, the 'golden section', which has a ratio of 1:1.618. Certain combinations found within the Fibonacci sequence also produce proportions very close to that of the golden section; for example, 3:5, 5:8 and 21:34. Formats common to us today, such as the DIN 'A' series of paper sizes, are commonly mistaken as containing the same proportions as the golden section, but in reality have the ratio 1:1.414.

Whilst not strictly grid systems, familiarity in working with traditional proportions and ratios for determining page size and text area dimensions can be rewarding. It is no coincidence that many artists and designers alike have discovered and used such systems within their work. Furthermore, many of the proportions relate directly to nature, and so appear pleasing to the eye as they are already familiar to us, albeit subconsciously.

Traditional grids

Technically, there is no such thing as a 'traditional' grid, although guides were created to determine the proportions of margin and text areas relative to the page in early books. This can be clearly seen in early manuscripts, where scribes would mark out margins, columns and guides for each line of writing. Gutenberg's first printed Bible emulates the visual style of the manuscript and also the division of space and proportion. We could therefore argue that traditional grids were those developed and produced for book design, whether printed or found in manuscripts.

When considering proportion of page, text area and margins in relation to book design, the principles of Tschichold's 'canons' for proportions of 2:3 and 3:4 allow for flexible adaptations to other formats too.

Opposite
Classical proportion and order can be found in many older book pages.

Above
In classical book proportions, the relationship of the page size to margins and text area width and height to page size can be determined.

Opposite
The influence of Swiss
graphic design and
the pioneering work
toward grid systems
from the likes of Josef
Müller-Brockmann still
resonate today. Here an
eight column grid has
been used to help give
structure to this poster.

Modern grids

It is impossible to say where and
when exactly the modern grid was
developed and established in terms
of graphic design and typography.
In many ways, development of the
grid was (and still is) an evolutionary
process. Early and later modernist
design schools in mainland Europe
explored the possibilities of the grid
through art and design.

One major influence was the architect
Le Corbusier's 'Modulor', a system
of proportion and division based
upon the golden section and human
proportion. This system of seemingly
endless possibility based its divisions
of space on human height, the height
of the raised arm, the height of the
solar plexus and the height from the
floor to the crotch. The use of the
human figure in Le Corbusier's system
makes sense as people will use and fill
the spaces created by the architect;
but Le Corbusier also demonstrated
how the grid could be applied to the
printed page too.

It is the work from Zurich, Basel and
Ulm in the 1950s and 60s that perhaps
influenced the world to incorporate the
use of the grid within graphic design.

Designers such as Joseph Müller-
Brockmann and Karl Gerstner took
this further still with their manifestos
and theories of the grid, its use and
application. These became manuals
for methodologies of producing and
working with grid systems, from the
division of horizontal and vertical space
relative to the page and areas for text
and image matter, to the metaphysical
concept of the grid as a programme or
holistic discipline that could be used
for problem-solving in design.

Consideration of the use of grids
within typographic design work must
relate to both the content and the
context of the work to be produced.
It is impossible to prescribe at which
point in the design process a grid
system should be introduced. This
will be towards the earlier stages of
the process certainly, but perhaps not
before the initial concept is worked
through. This may take some working
backwards and forwards between the
overall design concept in relation to
rationalizing aspects of the design
such as the choice of typeface and line
length. The latter will give an indication
as to dimensions for column widths of
the grid, for example. Remember, the
design should take priority – the grid
must be used to *guide*, not
to *constrain*.

Exhibition, symposium, public lecture and workshop

coll3ct
cultures of collecting

Cultures of collecting
From Girls Aloud memorabilia to a collection of faults, from fanzines to a cabinet of curios, this unique exhibition reveals an individual approach to a personally chosen set of objects. Many of us might consider objects as companions to our emotional lives; they may be provocations for others to make connections and the conversations they hold when viewed become the starting point for more discussion. Do objects and collections speak?

Private view
Monday 7 March
5pm to 7pm

Open to the public
Monday to Friday
7 March to 4 April
10am to 4pm
Admission free

Eldon Building
Winston Churchill Avenue
Portsmouth PO1 2DJ

Symposium
Cultures of Collecting
Wednesday 23 March
1pm to 5.45pm

Eldon Building
Winston Churchill Avenue
Portsmouth PO1 2DJ

Public lecture
Wednesday 23 March
7pm to 8.30pm

Park Building
King Henry Street
Portsmouth PO1 2DZ

Workshop
Meet the Exhibitors
Thursday 24 March
10am to 1pm

City Museum
Museum Road
Portsmouth PO1 2LJ

Booking required
Denise Callender
T +44 (0)23 9284 5137
denise.callender@port.ac.uk

Further details
Symposium, workshop and
public lecture, visit
www.port.ac.uk/research/
coart/collect3

Exhibiters
Jan Adams
Dr Jackie Berry
Denise Callender
Jane Chandler
John O'Keeran
Mark Eyles
Hilde Hollaaa
Professor George Hardie
Professor Sue Harper
Jody Harrison
Michelle Littlewood
Jacqui Muir
Dr Maureen O'Neill
Martin Robinson-Dowland
Alan Wood

Symposium speakers
Dr Jenny Walden
Dr Paul Martin
Martin Robinson-Dowland
Professor George Hardie
Dr Patricia Skinner
Rhiannon Williams
Dr Teddy Gebir

Public lecture
Rosamund Hardinge

Workshop
Dr Jenny Walden
Alison Carter
Norris Walker

Types of grid

A few examples of basic grid types are described here, but you should research and develop these in relation to your own work to find practical applications to given design problems.

Simple typographic grids

These may consist simply of a number of vertical columns used to position text and image matter, and may include the space between columns – the gutters – and the margins of the page, which must be given consideration. It may be necessary to produce grids with narrower sub-columns to enable a greater degree of flexibility in the design and layout of pages. Text widths can be set to multiples of the narrower columns, allowing the design to accommodate different matter thus allowing for a change of pace, rhythm and style from one page or section to the next, while still relating the content.

Modular grids

Modular grids are associated with Swiss typography or the 'International Style' of the 1950s and 60s (see also page 99). As well as a vertical division of space, modular grids divide space horizontally too, creating units or cells. The depth of the cell may depend upon the size of the text type and leading being used. Multiples of the line depth (leading size) form a good basis on which to construct the cells.

For example, ten lines of 10pt type on 12pt leading could allow for a cell height of 120pt within the grid. Again, each cell division is spaced by the equivalent of a gutter both vertically and horizontally. Vertical columns still appear, but further rationalization as to the position of text and image in relation to the depth of the page can be made via the grid.

Symmetric grids

Symmetric grids sit centrally on a single page (folio) so that the left and right margins are equal. The term can also be applied to a grid system used across facing pages where the position of the margins and text areas are symmetrically reflected or mirrored. Margins are not necessarily equal but run both left and right of the text area on single pages and are mirrored across the spread.

Asymmetric grids

These grids may have an off-centre appearance either as single pages or combined in spreads. If used in spreads, the grid is not mirrored from one page to the next as in symmetrical grids, but is more likely to appear repeated in a single position from page to page. Again, as with all grid systems, attention to the relationship of the margins is important. It can be this element alone that determines the success of the eventual layout.

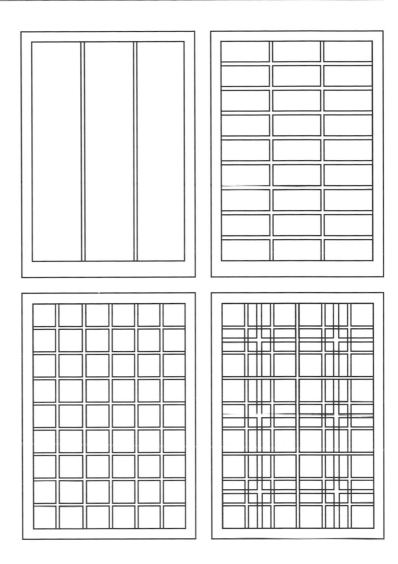

Above
Grids are often
constructed as simple
columns of vertical lines
but may be devised as
more complex modular
systems allowing for
greater flexibility.

Baseline grids

Baseline grids allow for an extra level of control within the typographic layout. Using a baseline grid is most useful for controlling line spacing and the alignment of text or body copy within a design. It is the value for the leading of the type that is used to specify the distance between lines of the baseline grid. For example, if we were to use 10pt Times type with 12pt leading, then the 12pt measurement for the leading would be the value that would be set for the baseline grid.

Like all grid systems, the baseline grid is not used to dictate the development of the design, but is rather used as an aid to help with consistency within the work. This kind of grid is particularly beneficial when dealing with lots of text and when using multiple columns. The baseline grid makes the alignment of columns across a spread and throughout a publication an easier and more accurate task. This is sometimes referred to as 'cross-alignment'. Industry standard software programs allow baseline grids to be created simply, usually within the 'preferences' menu. These grids can be set up to coincide with margins that may be created and type can be 'snapped to' the baseline grid, automating part of the alignment process also.

The reason for using the leading measurement relating to the text type size is that this usually forms the bulk of the typographic matter that the designer will work with, especially within publication design. It is also very difficult and time-consuming to align small type sizes optically, whilst maintaining a high degree of accuracy.

Other typographic elements within the layout can be aligned to the baseline grid, such as running heads, headings, subheadings, standfirsts and so on. It may be worthwhile considering using multiples or divisions of the specified leading of the text matter when deciding on sizes for other type elements. For example, 22pt Times on 24pt leading would allow for alignment of this baseline on every second line of the 12pt baseline grid of the text.

In short, the baseline grid should allow for multiples to develop. Again, using the example of the 10pt Times on 12pt leading, a 6pt baseline grid would mean that the type sits on every second line, but it may also allow for greater flexibility in dealing with small text matter such as captions and footnotes. Remember, the baseline grid should not dictate the development of the design, but should rather be seen as a virtual typographic safety net for the text matter.

level one design series

'Who needs
grid anywa...
If it looks
right, it is
right. Righ...

structure in the page

Baseline grid by Michael Harkins

Here we will take a look at some of the fundamentals of
publication design. These processes and working methods
can apply to newspaper design, designing brochures, book
design – in fact essential information that every graphic
designer should be aware of.

...ign series

...e volor iusciliquis do et
...sequis er sequipsusto
...venit niam digna adipit
...exero consequam, senis
...nummodo delit la aut
...n nostrud tetummodip
...d ming eugait in hent
...estio odolore duissecte
...oloreet doloreetum.

...huisis duiscil el ing erat.
...mconsed modolor eraeseq
...sed te vent lorperit ulla
...in hent alisl et ipit dolor
...is at, sisit, vel dignim dunt
...sto odo od euguerostrud

facidunt venim zzriliq uationsequi...
et nulla am ercinisci exercilis euga...
esequatie magnism oluptat ute con...
tatie magniat aut ea faciduis alit at...
estionu llandrem quam iustinim iri...
mincipsumsan utpat ip eum dionse...

Above
The diagram shows
a 12pt baseline grid
set for a double-page
spread working in
conjunction with a
six-column grid. Type
and leading values of
varying sizes relating
to the baseline grid are
used for the different
elements in the layout.

Left
This detail shows
how the baseline grid
helps with alignment
(cross-alignment) of the
baselines across text
columns and additional
type matter.

Find the grid

Grid systems are used in graphic design to enable us to deal with what is sometimes complex information in a systematic and precise manner. They can bring order, clarity and hierarchy to visual communication. They can also help us to develop our design concepts further if handled appropriately.

The task

Find three different examples of grids in use in graphic design. These may not be obvious at first. They could be found within the page layout of a book, newspaper or magazine. You may find grid systems within the design of corporate identities or information design. Once you have found your chosen grid systems, analyze these.

- Using tracing paper (or typo-detail paper), mark out the found existing grid structure.

- Record sizes of margins, the number and widths of columns, gutter widths and so on.

- Determine whether the grid is symmetric or asymmetric.

- Does the grid use a modular cell-like structure?

- Make it clear that you understand the structure of your chosen grid systems.

Understanding how and where grid systems are used is helpful in determining how to employ them within your own work. Remember: grid systems provide a flexible, invisible framework for typographic design.

Tip

If you find that you are only drawing around blocks of text and images without identifying the underlying structure, then you need to look a little further.

If you identify a grid system within a page of a publication, check to see if it fits with other pages. Also, is it mirrored on the facing pages or not?

Above

Pictured above is Experimental Jetset's '10 years of posters' exhibition which took place at Kemistry Gallery in London. Clear, unstructured simplicity, combined with thoughtful, clever concepts underpins the work shown here.

RYDE, I.W.

MESSRS.

WALLIS, RIDDETT & DOWN

WILL SELL BY AUCTION ON THE PREMISES,

ON THURSDAY, OCTOBER 27, 1887,

And following day if necessary, commencing at TWELVE o'clock punctually,

THE VALUABLE

CONTENTS

OF

PALMER HOUSE,

CASTLE STREET, RYDE.

Being the appointments of Four Reception Rooms, Ten Bed and Dressing Rooms, and including:

A HANDSOME MAHOGANY PEDESTAL SIDEBOARD,

Lounge Chair and Twelve smaller Chairs in Morocco Leather,

Extending Dining Table, an old Mahogany Cellaret, Couches, Lounge Chairs, Bookcases and other

WALNUT & ROSEWOOD DRAWING ROOM FURNITURE

Of superior quality, Brussels and Tapestry Carpets, Set of three bronze and ormolu Candelabra, with crystal mounts,

ANTIQUE CLOCKS AND VALUABLE ORNAMENTS,

A ROSEWOOD SECRETAIRE,

EXCELLENT MAHOGANY BEDROOM FURNITURE,

INCLUDING:

Five Good Wardrobes, Twenty Washstands and Dressing Tables,

And several Chests of Drawers.

Iron and Mahogany Bedsteads,

Eleven Feather Beds and other Bedding, Sets of Chamber Ware, Painted Furniture, Window Furnitures of crimson Rep and Damask, Mantel Glasses, Dinner and Dessert Services, the usual appointments of the Kitchen and Offices and various other Effects.

May be Viewed on the preceding day.   Catalogues may be had at the Auctioneers' Offices, Ryde.

The House to be Let, Unfurnished: apply to the Auctioneers.

We can think of typography as comprising of two
main areas – text typography and display typography.
We have already discovered that some designers
refer to micro and macro qualities of typography. These
two broad definitions may encompass slightly different
things but they ultimately involve considerations of
the overall appearance of a typographic composition,
including layout, balance, structure and hierarchy.

There is also the detail of typography to take into
consideration; legibility, readability, the size of the text
type, word and letter-spacing, line length, leading (the
space between lines of type) and many other such small
refinements. This chapter discusses some of the general
points associated with these two broad definitions.

Opposite
Shown here is
Experimental Jetset's
poster for 'Helvetica',
a documentary film
by Gary Hustwit.
Considered to be both
a text and display
typeface, Helvetica's
ubiquity has earned it a
great deal of attention
and perhaps a certain
notoriety according to
some designers.

Text typography

So what exactly is meant by text typography? Text typography is typography that is intended for continuous reading. It is usually the kind of typography that most of us take for granted. We are so used to looking at it that we just don't see it. Reading books, newspapers, magazines and web pages all rely on a considered use of typefaces intended for text settings. Most people don't even consider that the typefaces themselves have been designed – they are just there for us to read. But this doesn't happen merely by accident.

Type designers are aware of problems caused by type that is too conspicuous. If we are too conscious of the style, shape and size of the letters within a text this becomes distracting. Although there are thousands of text typefaces that we might use in our typography – many of which appear highly individual on closer inspection – there are some general key points to look for when selecting and using text types.

As a general guide, text type should normally appear somewhere between around 8pt and 14pt for continuous reading, depending on the typeface used. Smaller sizes may be used for captions (here type of approximately 6pt is a commonly used size). Above 14pt, the text appears very large, and will usually be difficult to read within the pages of a book, magazine or newspaper. These sizes are given only for guidance, as factors such as whether you choose a serif or sans serif typeface will also have an impact on the size of type you choose, as we will discuss in more detail in chapter four.

'Type, the voice of the printed page, can be legible and dull, or legible and fascinating, according to its design and treatment.'
Paul Beaujon (Beatrice Warde)
The Monotype Recorder, Vol. 32, No. 1. 1933

Meet the cast:

ABCD EFGHIJK LMNOP QRSTUV WXYZ

Now see the movie:

Helvetica

A documentary film by Gary Hustwit

A Swiss Dots
production,
in association
with **Veer**

swiss
dots

Helvetica
A documentary film
by Gary Hustwit

Featuring:
Michael Bierut
Neville Brody
Matthew Carter
David Carson
Wim Crouwel
Experimental Jetset
Tobias Frere-Jones
Otmar Hoefer
Jonathan Hoefler
Alfred Hoffmann

Lars Müller
Norm
Mike Parker
Michael C. Place
Rick Poynor
Stefan Sagmeister
Leslie Savan
Paula Scher
Manfred Schulz
Erik Spiekermann
Bruno Steinert

Massimo Vignelli
Hermann Zapf

**Produced and
Directed by**
Gary Hustwit

Editor:
Shelby Siegel

helveticafilm.com

**Director of
Photography:**
Luke Geissbühler

**Additional
Photography:**
Colin Brown
Gary Hustwit
Pete Sillen
Chris Wetton
Ben Wolf

Additional Editing:
Laura Weinberg

Sound Editor:
Brian Langman

Sound Mixer:
Andy Kris

Motion Graphics:
Trollbäck & Co.

**Sound
Recording:**
Nara Garber
Victor Horstink
Dan Johnson
Jörg Kidowski
Sam Pullen
Reto Stamm

Poster by
Experimental Jetset

Music:
The Album Leaf
Battles
Caribou
Chicago Underground
Quartet
El Ten Eleven
Four Tet
Kim Hiorthøy
Motohiro Nakashima
Sam Prekop

**Associate
Producers:**
Andrew Dreskin
John Goldsmith
Sharon Hustwit
Michelle Hustwit
Jakob Trollbäck
Antoine Wilson
Chris Levinson Wilson

(c) 2007 Swiss Dots

Basic considerations

For any lengthy text setting, readability and legibility of the type must be of first importance. You may want to use serif or sans serif types. You will find lots of interesting fonts that you do want to use, but consider them in a little more detail if they are to be used for text settings. Do they have a good x-height? Are the counters and bowls (the spaces within the letters) clearly visible? Do the proportions of the ascenders and descenders look clear and well considered in relation to the x-height? If the typeface has a vertical or horizontal stress to the design, is the relationship between the thick and thin strokes well balanced? Do the width of the letters look well balanced, or are these too narrow or too wide? Does the typeface appear too heavy or does it look too light?

When selecting text type, it is important to test what you have selected. This really is the only way you will know if the type is going to work. When using the computer, we have a tendency to zoom in and zoom out of our work, which often gives us the false impression that everything will look okay. Of course, this is fine if you are designing a web page, as what you see on screen is what you will get, just as long as the user's web browser can support the fonts that you have selected.

Designing for print, however, requires looking at type at the size (and form) that this will appear in the finished job. The only way to do this is to produce hard copies (print-outs). You may need to make several of these as you make corrections and decisions as to what seems to be working and what isn't. With practice, you can train your eye to see how small differences in your choices and decisions actually have a big effect on the overall design. This takes us back again to the relationship between micro and macro typography!

You should also bear in mind what the work is for and who the intended audience may be. For example, you wouldn't expect type within a children's book to be very small or overly decorative if the intended purpose of the book is to help children to learn to read. Likewise, you wouldn't imagine a serious book on philosophy to be set in a typeface more appropriate to comic books. Be careful not to get too carried away by your personal tastes or preferences. Finally, don't select fonts just because of their names! Choose them, print them, test them – do they read well? And are they appropriate for the job?

Above left
Type specimen books,
whether old or new,
can provide a wealth of
inspiration, as well as
enabling us to become
both more familiar
and critical in the type
choices that we make.

Above right
Gerard Unger's
specimen of his
newspaper text
typefaces demonstrates
a robustness and
ingenuity in their design.

Right
Collectively, serif text
types can appear to
have similar properties
in terms of weight or
colour. There is a certain
evenness in their design.
No one thing obviously
stands out.

Baskerville
Bell MT
Adobe Caslon Pro
Centuary
Garamond
Adobe Garamond Pro
Minion Pro
Palatino
Pedant Regular
Times New Roman

Display typography

Display typography, unlike text typography, is not usually intended for reading at length. Display typography draws our attention to certain parts of the page or design. It can act as signposting, guiding the eye across and through a design. It can help create clarity, hierarchy and order. It can add character, inform us, enthral us, enthuse us and sometimes purposefully confuse us or stop us in our tracks.

Display typography can be considered macrotypography, although some micro-adjustments may need to be made at times. From simple headings to complex deconstructive compositions, display typography provides more in terms of typographic image. Display typography can also become image or image-like, depending on how far it is taken and how confidently a designer works with it.

Types to use in display settings and compositions are afforded greater variation than those that will work successfully at text size. However, quite often, text types can be enlarged and still work perfectly well, as the minutiae of detail may look very pleasing at display sizes. Many text font families will have specially drawn 'display' or 'titling' variants. These are intended to appear at larger sizes and may have thinner stems and strokes or ascenders and descenders of different length; or the serifs may be smaller in proportion to their text-based siblings. These small changes can prevent the type appearing too heavy or bulky, or make its proportions appear more harmonious, especially when greatly increased in size.

If text types are introverted or conservative by nature, the same does not hold true for display types; some of these are most definitely extroverts – perhaps even exhibitionists! In terms of appearance, these can range from the classical to the crass and from the sublime to the ridiculous. In short, anything goes when it comes to display types. This is not to say that taste should be neglected, though.

Left
The display typography
in the lettering used
here for the Pozza
Palace in Dubrovnik
by Phil Baines and
Catherine Dixon takes
on image-like qualities.

Attention to detail

There is much more potential for expression when selecting and working with display types. However, it is possible that the display typography will be the most immediately noticeable aspect of your design, so it will need to be given the same care and consideration as text typography; or more so, as in some cases it is the display type that is most likely to remain in people's minds. Try to avoid clichéd or obvious visual associations. The car mechanic down the road doesn't need a typeface assembled from spanners – you get the idea.

Again, if text typography is 'invisible' to most of us, display type is the opposite. This is the kind of typography that most of us are used to seeing. Because display types can vary so much in terms of their design, it may not be completely necessary to be so concerned regarding factors such as proportions of x-height, width of character and so on as you would when considering text types.

As with text type, however, ensure that you test, experiment and look at print-outs. Compare your choice of display type with what you consider successful work produced by other designers – but try not to mimic or pastiche their designs. As before, ensure that your choice is appropriate for its purpose.

Below
The bespoke
display typeface and
typography accentuates
the title in this
exhibition catalogue
for Psycho Buildings at
the Hayward Gallery,
London (2008) by
A2 Design.

YCHO ILDINGS

ARTISTS TAKE ON
ARCHITECTURE

ATELIER BOW-WOW
MICHAEL BEUTLER
GELITIN
LOS CARPINTEROS
MIKE NELSON
ERNESTO NETO
TOBIAS PUTRIH
TOMAS SARACENO
DO HO SUH
RACHEL WHITEREAD

'The typographer ...who did not hit upon the specially
appropriate type, will not have done actual harm to the
transmission of the meaning of the text, but missed an
opportunity to intensify the force of impression of the text... '

G. W. Ovink

Words, lines and paragraphs

Typography deals essentially with the arrangement of words, lines of words and groups of lines to form paragraphs. This might seem obvious, but there is a lot to consider when designing with type – perhaps more than first meets the eye.

Some researchers believe that we don't read words letter by letter, but that we tend to identify words by their outline or overall shape. This is particularly true of type set in upper and lower case. The differentiation of heights of the x-height, ascenders and descenders helps to produce distinctive and recognisable word shapes when letters are grouped together.

So it is no mistake that most of what we read, especially that intended for continuous or extended reading, is (and should be) set in upper and lower case. This gives more chance of creating memorable word shapes. Other studies identify aspects of individual letters within words that may help us when reading.

Words

Whatever the science, it is generally considered that words set in upper and lower case are more readable than those set in upper case only. Setting type as upper case not only produces less in terms of recognizable word shapes, but there is also a loss of rhythm created between letters.

Upper-case letters form more regular patterns and also need to be spaced more widely than do lower-case letters to help with readability. Conversely, increasing the space between lower-case letters breaks up this rhythm and reduces readability.

Words set in upper case may be useful in display settings and titles. It can also prove useful to give emphasis with upper-case words, though this should be executed with care, especially in text settings. Single words set in upper case can often look too large in text-size settings, so consider the use of italics or small caps for these instances.

Single words or collections of words used in display typography can breathe life into a design. The relationship between the meaning of a word and its placement, colour and choice of type can produce some very interesting results, even in the simplest of designs. Care will need to be given to size, weight and the spacing of letters.

Opposite
The relationship of letters, the space between letters, words and word-spacing, lines and line-spacing, all contribute towards the creation of successful and pleasing typography.

Wordshape WORDSHAPE Wordshape

If lines of type are set too long or too short, it can either become difficult for the reader to locate the next line in a paragraph (particularly when there is extended reading matter to consider), or the text can appear broken and interrupted. The setting should take into account letter-spacing, word-spacing and inter-linear spacing (leading). Each of these elements will have an influence not just on the overall appearance of the text, but also on how the text functions. It is important to recognise that text typography and display typography require different levels of attention to detail also. This is not to say that similar issues will not apply in each case. It may be however, that certain details become more or less apparent depending upon the application of the type.

If lines of type are set too long or too short, it can either become difficult for the reader to locate the next line in a paragraph (particularly when there is extended reading matter to consider), or the text can appear broken and interrupted. The setting should take into account letter-spacing, word-spacing and inter-linear spacing (leading). Each of these elements will have an influence not just on the overall appearance of the text, but also on how the text functions. It is important to recognise that text typography and display typography require different levels of attention to detail also. This is not to say that similar issues will not apply in each case. It may be however, that certain details become more or less apparent depending upon the application of the type.

If lines of type are set too long or too short, it can either become difficult for the reader to locate the next line in a paragraph (particularly when there is extended reading matter to …

If lines of type are set too long or too short, it can either become difficult for the reader to locate the next line in a paragraph (particularly when there is extended reading matter to consider), or the text can appear broken and interrupted. The setting should take into account letter-spacing, word-spacing and inter-linear spacing (leading). Each of these elements will have an influence not just on the overall appearance of the text, but also on how the text functions.

If lines of type are set too long or too short, it can either become difficult …

Early Years Foundation Stage The welfare of the child is paramount Unique Child United Nations convention on children's rights Children's act 1989 Positive relationships Parents as partners Early years professionals Learning through play Indoor and outdoor play Self confidence and self esteem Behaviour and self control Risk and challenge Health and well being Healthy eating Breakfast club After school club Snack cafe School lunches exploration and investigation Safety and dignity Multi agency working in partnership Special educational needs Equality and diversity Community Rights and responsibilities Respect for ourselves and others …

Lines

Lines of type must be given special consideration, depending on how they will be used. In display typography, lines of type must consider not only the spacing of letters but also the spacing between words. This may become more apparent and begin to look too large when the type size is increased. Obviously, this will depend upon the typeface used too. Often, typefaces designed specifically for display purposes will compensate to some extent for this, but really this is a job for the eye, and one that the designer needs to be aware of.

Lines of type set at text sizes will define text area widths. This may be in relation to the widths of columns within a grid system, for example, or the text area of a book. It is important that the line length for text setting is defined and is appropriate for the design. Think about the difference between the length of the lines of type that you find when reading a novel compared to those in newspapers or magazines. Each work in specific ways and differently affect how we read. Letter spacing and word spacing are most important in creating the effect of an even line of type, that is, one that doesn't disturb the eye.

Paragraphs

At larger display sizes, paragraphs tend to work as single lines of type. Attention must be given to the spacing between lines (leading), and again this may behave very differently at display size in comparison to text sizes. Often, the leading between lines will need to be reduced at larger sizes if the shape of the paragraph is to be maintained.

At text sizes, the paragraph forms a visual block, which must be given consideration not only as an element within the overall design (macrotypography), but also as part of the choice of typeface, type size, letter spacing, word spacing, line length and leading, which will all have a bearing on how the paragraph appears too. The alignment of type in a paragraph will also have an impact on readability and on the look of the design.

Many designers prefer to range paragraphs left to give even word spacing. New paragraphs should be separated with a line space, half line space, or be indented. If indenting, these should be kept together (with no line space) and the indent should ideally be the width of one em (of the same value as the type size in use). The first paragraph in a chapter or section should not be indented unless using an initial drop capital.

Opposite
This sample of the author's work is concerned with the breaking of conventions and shows text type working as display type and image simultaneously.

Anatomy of the page

Just as it is important to understand the language of typography that describes the precise characteristics of letters, the parts of letters, and the space inside and between letters, as well as to understand words, paragraphs and arrangement, it is just as important to think about typography in terms of how and where it is specifically applied. This includes considerations particular or peculiar to certain kinds of artefacts.

The typographic page in print can be considered in its simplest form as one side of a piece of paper. A single page may be referred to as a 'folio' (particularly in book work) and two facing pages as a 'spread' or sometimes as a 'double-page spread' (DPS), as in magazine design. Facing pages in book design are also referred to in terms of the 'verso' (left page) and 'recto' (right page).

In publication design (for example, book, magazine, newspaper and brochure design), the page is often divided into text and marginal areas. Margins for publications are often referred to as the head (top), foot (bottom), fore-edge (outside) and back (inside or towards the spine). Margins may contain other typographic matter in support of the main text itself, such as notes. Captions, running heads or footers, folios (page numbers) and other typographic devices may also be included.

Single page designs (where unbound) use the terms 'left margin' and 'right margin' as opposed to 'fore-edge' and 'back'.

The 'text area' may be of a single width or divided into columns or 'cells' (as described previously in the section on Grid systems on pp.60–69). Although there are many ways to divide the typographic space, as a broad rule, the 'foot' margin is always made proportionally larger than others; otherwise the text area will appear too low on the page. This problem of optical balance is also encountered when determining the vertical centre of a page, whether in single pages or spreads. The optical centre is always slightly higher than the mathematical centre, the latter appearing too low also.

Opposite top
Page anatomy relative to a spread.

Opposite bottom
Optical factors must be considered alongside mathematical measurement.

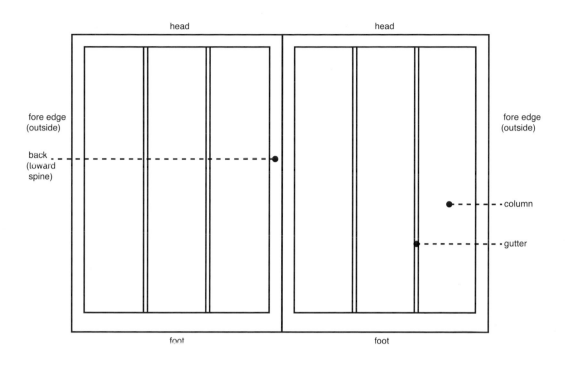

head head

fore edge
(outside)

fore edge
(outside)

back
(toward
spine)

column

gutter

foot foot

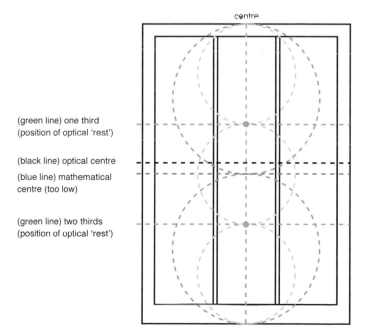

centre

(green line) one third
(position of optical 'rest')

(black line) optical centre

(blue line) mathematical
centre (too low)

(green line) two thirds
(position of optical 'rest')

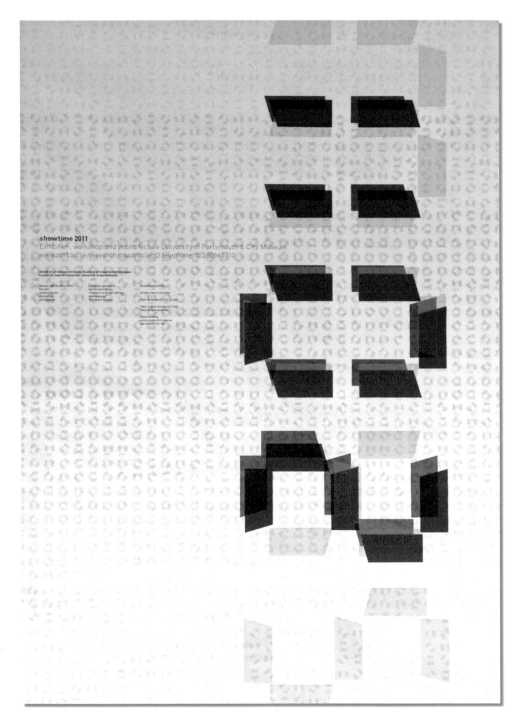

Poster

Occasionally referred to as a 'broadside' or 'broadsheet', posters in many cases are printed on one side only (although this is not exclusively the case). The typographic poster requires some special consideration, not just in terms of what audience it will appeal to, but also in terms of where the poster will be seen and from what kinds of distances. Typography may have to work on several different levels, not only in terms of hierarchy but also in terms of scale. If the poster is to be seen from a distance, it may be necessary to render type at large sizes in order to 'draw in' the viewer. Conversely, if you know that the poster will also be viewed at close range (for example, if it contains a detailed list of times and events), the overly large type will appear less clear and easy to read at close proximity.

Identity

In terms of type and items of standard corporate identity – letterheads and business cards – it is important to recognize current conventions and norms, in addition to trying to create something new and exciting when designing. The majority of international letterhead paper conforms to the ISO/DIN A4 format of 297 × 210mm (with the main exceptions of USA letter 8 ¼" × 11 ¾" and Canada's P4 format 215 × 280mm). Care must be given to allow adequate room in the left-hand margin for filing (usually 20–25mm), and also to ensure that the letter can fold into different envelope formats (such as DL 2 folds and C4 single folds) whilst allowing the recipient's address to be viewed through the envelope window.

Business cards usually (though not exclusively) conform to the standard credit card sizes of 55 × 85mm. This is for practical reasons more than for anything else. They fit nicely into wallets and purses, which is important in business terms.

Opposite
This poster, created by the author, is designed to be read from both near and far. The design also works through the poster, due to the translucent paper used.

Book

In addition to considerations of proportion for the marginal and text areas, book design requires some serious consideration in terms of how the content influences decisions made in relation to the use of the text area.

Books that have only continuous text matter for their content may provide more obvious examples in terms of the division of the typographic page into margins and text area. This will still include margins used to contain running heads, footers and folios. The book itself will also divide into sections of prelims or front matter, text matter (the main body of the book) and end matter. Continuous text matter may be set to a single measure (width), as in novels, for example, or to several columns in cases where the book itself is of a large size.

Short, in-depth content matter, such as that found in dictionaries and encyclopedias, tends to be set in columns as this allows for easier access to and retrieval of information.

Textbooks may often have a fairly comprehensive grid system to allow for the variety of content that they contain and in order to accommodate the variations in configuring text and image matter that this may necessitate. Margins may also be reduced to a minimum in cases where the amount of information to be included is given precedence over the considerations of 'white space', for example.

A typical book construction may contain the following elements:

cover
endpaper
the bastard title page
            (often mistaken for half-title)
frontispiece
title page
copyright and imprint
dedication
acknowledgements
foreword
preface
contents
list of illustrations
introduction
half-title page

main body of text

end matter
appendix
glossary
bibliography
index
endpaper
cover

In some cases, the order may change slightly and in many modern books much of the front matter is often greatly reduced.

Right

This page from the Borough Market Cookbook, designed by Catherine Dixon, shows how subtle hierarchy creates a balanced 'textbook'-style page.

Below

In this book, Paulus M. Dreibholz has used italics to capture the essence of conversation between interviewer and interviewee.

JAMAICAN JERK WILD BOAR
LOIN CHOPS WITH AVOCADO
AND MELON SALAD

Don't be put off by the long list of ingredients for the marinade, as you probably have them lurking in the back of your pantry. Peter Gott's boar chops have enough flavour to stand up to this classic Caribbean dish. Each of the chops has a bit of the loin, along with a piece of the boar fillet. These chops are delicious served with roast sweet potatoes – or better yet, roast sweet potato buttermilk cornbread. [S.L.B]

Preparation time 15 minutes,
plus minimum 4 hours marinating

Cooking time 25 minutes

Serves 6

Season With the melon, fresh coriander and mint, this is best made in July when melons from Spain are ripe and juicy and the herbs most vibrant.

6 wild boar chops (bone-in)
1½ tsp ground allspice
1½ tsp dried thyme
¾ tsp cayenne pepper
¾ tsp freshly ground black pepper
½ tsp freshly ground nutmeg
½ tsp cinnamon
9 garlic cloves
Sea salt
1 jalapeno chilli
5 spring onions
1 lime (juice only) plus 1 or 2 more (enough for 3 tblsp juice)
50ml olive oil plus 1 tblsp
50ml soy sauce
2 oranges (enough for 120ml juice)
1 large avocado
½ cantaloupe melon
1 small red onion
15g fresh mint
15g fresh coriander

Begin by marinating the loin chops. Mix the dried herbs and spices together in a small bowl. Peel and crush the garlic cloves with a little salt with a pestle and mortar. Wash and blot dry the chilli and spring onion. Cut the chilli in half and remove the seeds. Chop off the root end and peel off the outer layer of the spring onions. Slice both the chilli and spring onions and add to the pestle and mortar with the garlic, pounding the three ingredients together into a paste. Add to the spice bowl. Squeeze the oranges and lime and add the juice to the spice bowl along with the olive oil and soy sauce. Place the boar chops in a glass baking dish and pour over the marinade. Cover and refrigerate for a minimum 4 hours but preferably overnight.

To cook the boar loin chops preheat the oven to 180°C / 350°F / gas 4.

Heat a little oil over a medium flame in a large ovenproof frying pan. Add the chops to the frying pan (you will have to do this in two pans or in batches) and cook until golden brown, about 7 minutes. Flip and transfer the pan to the oven. Bake until the chops are crisp on the outside and thermometer inserted into the meat registers 65.5°C / 150°F – about 18–20 minutes.

Once you have the boar in the oven, dice the flesh of both the avocado and melon. Peel and finely chop the red onion. Wash the mint, remove the leaves from the sprigs, and chop finely. The skinny stems of coriander are fine to add to the salad, but make sure that you clean the coriander thoroughly as it can be a bit sandy. Combine all these ingredients together with the 3 tblsp lime juice and 1 tblsp olive oil, plus a good seasoning of salt and freshly ground black pepper.

Serve the chops on warm plates with a little salsa on top.

SILLFIELD FARM   39

---

spaces, and you will find works that deal with the cultural translation of natural strata once scientifically and then artistically in. The perspectives are left empty as a way to confront the viewer with the void represented by the valley.

To conclude, we would like you to bear in mind that there is another platform that we've conceived and that is the publication, which is a book entitled Danger to Fall in the Sea which implies the Mediterranean as a subtext, something about which we were often questioned while travelling around Italy.

Well, while visiting Napoli we decided to go to Capri in the conquest of seeing Villa Malaparte, where Godard filmed Le Mépris. Our reading of the void, visually represented as the sea, resembled yet another of Benjamin's metaphors in his text 'The Concept of History', where he metaphorically describes historical materialism as the feeling of being overwhelmed by the amount of information, experienced by Klee's Angel painting; in which this figure is completely surprised with its eyes and wings wide open because it's shocked by the responsibility of having to engage with everything that has happened in the past. This reference to Benjamin and again the subject of the sea is basically one of the core structures of this publication, which includes texts and quotes by for example Rosalind Krauss, who in her essay 'The Optical Unconscious' takes the sea as a metaphor of modernity's obsessions with abstraction. For Krauss Mondrian's representations of the sea is like the unlimited gesture of the modern gaze towards that void which, is precisely the unrepresentable formless ocean. Our publication will also include excerpts by Italo Calvino and also by other artists who are not in the exhibition, such as Ciro Vitale, who is working on photographs taken by his grandfather when he was fighting in the colonial war in Ethiopia, as well as Maria Adele Del Vecchio and Meris Angioletti.

IB *The second discussion table will be presided by Francesco Bonami, our Artistic Director and also curator for the Biennale of 2010. Discussion will focus on the state of art in Italy on a more general basis. The question posed to the invited speakers was: Learning to be an artist? The reality of the Italian system.*

FRANCESCO BONAMI *Good afternoon. I'm Francesco Bonami Artistic Director at Fondazione Sandretto Re Rebaudengo. First of all I want to compliment the three curators and Ilaria Bonacossa for setting up this exhibition of Italian artists; it's a demonstration of how Italy is a prolific breeding ground yet to be discovered. The speakers at today's panel are Cristiana Collu, Director of MAN, Museum of contemporary art in Nuoro, then Anna Daneri, Martina Corgnati critic and art historian,*

Cristiana Perrella, Giacinto Di Pietrantonio and Marco Scotini.

The theme of today's roundtable is if it is possible to learn to be an artist. Can such discipline be taught or is one born an artist? Discussion will revolve on the reality of the Italian system. Two important issues are intertwined: the breeding ground for artists that are born from the various schools and centres and if the Italian system gives the opportunity to those who have studied art to actually become artists.

Is it possible to teach someone to be an artist, this question will be elaborated upon by our first speaker Cristiana Collu.

CRISTIANA COLLU *First of all thanks to Patrizia Sandretto for inviting me here today, usually I'm reluctant to accept these kinds of invitations but today marked an irresistible opportunity. Often my work leaves me in the backstage of a museum as a museum director, and when I'm invited to speak of these topics I tend to suffer from the 'impostor's' syndrome. Working in the geographical area where the MAN museum is located, that is the Barbagia, meaning the region of Sardinia, is a small cliché, giving me a too wide scope and, therefore, I'm not sure I can properly answer the issue on the Italian system and young artists. From personal experience a few features characterize my work, those being instinct, that some might attribute to the fact that I am a woman, and improvisation, that many would link to me being Italian thus making me an improviser by nature. This means flexibility and the ability of constructing without prejudices a new reality, and if one believes that the future arrives one day at a time, it has to be constructed in the present. Here in Guarene there are two aspects that I can relate to, the concept of identity and that of hospitality, two cliché well known in Sardinia that can be useful to describe the scenery for young artists today, whom are very close to the idea of identity, possibly to a certain individuality. Such does not come as a surprise considering the themes of our current society, as for instance homologation. In any case identity is not to be seen as occurs in Sardinia as a burden, but more as the starting point for a project; that is to become the future, and can perfectly be captured by young generations. Moreover, nowadays when the word 'crisis' is the catch word, one has to think of how in Chinese such word is composed by two symbols, one representing 'risk' and the other 'opportunity'. This makes investing in such work and taking on a risk, but also acquiring a new opportunity. The following quotes encapsulates what I'm hoping is the message to be followed, that of having faith towards new generations, which is something Patrizia Sandretto does and has consistently been doing... Alda Merini said: I wonder what is the link between past and modern times, nonetheless youth comes to us to help resolve their problems, even if we haven't resolved anything.' This is the message to be passed on to young artists and curators. Another quote still*

56   57

Magazines and newspapers

Magazines and newspapers share some common attributes in that the typographic space is usually divided into multiple columns or modular grid cells. Newspaper formats are perhaps less differentiated today. Many of the 'serious' newspapers have adopted the smaller tabloid format, which was once synonymous with the so-called 'popular' press.

Popular tabloids may still use space within their newspapers to grab attention, particularly with their covers. This gives a somewhat non-standard or undisciplined feel to the use of typography in many cases. In comparison, the more serious newspapers tend to espouse a very formal and rigorous approach to the relationship of type to space in their pages. Newspapers tend to be very text-intensive, so it is important to maximize the use of text to space. This may include a limited range of heading sizes, the formalized use of column widths for certain kinds of editorial and so on. White space – although evident – is only slight in most cases. Space is predominantly given over to news.

Magazines, in contrast to many newspapers, may make a feature of the relationship of white space to text and image matter. While perhaps still using a highly rationalized grid structure, magazine design may make statements in terms of lifestyle and choice by the way in which priority is given as much to the look of the editorial material in terms of style as it is to the content. The interaction of text typography, display typography, image and space can be far more dynamic and individual from feature to feature than that routinely found in newspaper design.

Exhibition

Typography and the space it occupies in exhibition design needs to be planned in terms of how the visitor or viewer of that information will interact with the space. Is there a sequence by which viewers are expected to view information? Is there a natural flow of footfall at the exhibition space?

Information should ideally be kept to the bare essentials. Keep it clear. Make sure that you are allowing readers of an average height to see information within their eye-line. A large block of text is no good at knee-height if set at 18pt. Make sure that lighting is adequate in the space. Small texts and certain colours in dimly lit environments make reading uncomfortable and sometimes impossible. Use size to draw viewers' attention, but remember to be directly sympathetic to the content or the exhibits themselves.

HEAD OF STUDIO PRIX

In our studio, the students are challenged to make unimaginable projects imaginable, and we teach them strategies which enable them to transform these imaginable projects into actual architecture. It is not about limiting ideas through objective constraints. On the contrary: We teach how to use objective constraints to construct architecture. Nowadays, it is not only radical thinking which is paramount. Radical architecture is produced when extraordinary buildings are both successfully presented and actually realized. That means on the one hand being well-versed in theoretical fields and on the other hand understanding politics.

The process of design is a process of thinking. Without a theoretical background, only unoriginal solutions can be found.

For this reason we find it important to analyse and critically assess the relationship between theory and reality. In this context, developing a new aesthetic based on societal influences should be placed in the foreground.

PRIX
WOLF D.

STUDIO PRIX—THEORY AND BACKGROUND, ES PORTFOLIO MANAGEMENT

Good evening, my name is Reiner Zettl and I teach in the studio of Prof. Prix but this evening I represent the postgraduate master program Urban Strategies. What

REINER
ZETTL

you see on the screen is an anticipation of the future that we think might happen between Vienna and Bratislava. I am sure you have heard of the Twin City. Although at the moment more a marketing claim than anything else, the name itself creates an awareness of potential development. It is a question of new maps,

and especially mental maps to restructure the existing perception of this territory in order to overcome mental blocks and barriers and to initiate a process that eventually might lead to a coalescence of the 2 cities. Scenarios should help to show in what way the wider context of politics, economy, and climate has an influence onto the area between ex- east and west and will define strategies to organize and coordinate the process of growth.

Besides the sociographic specificity of the task their is the general question about the future city. Its raison d'être in the age of ubiquitous information and communication beyond physical space, its relation to resources and to nature. What are the synergies between Bratislava and Vienna taking the Danube as a large central park?

The next program, as Mr Prix has announced will focus on urban densification.

Before starting I promised Mr Glaeser I would give him one minute of my time and therefore I stop now.

Thank you for your attention.

Information design

There is one important facet to bear in mind above all else when considering typography for information design, which is functionality. Because we usually experience information design when looking for something else, we tend not to see this as design. It can thus become the most invisible of typographic treatments.

Readability and legibility are very important considerations. Within diagrams, for example, the text must not overpower the appearance of the visualized information.

Although sans serif types may give a 'neutral' aesthetic tone compared to many serif typefaces, this doesn't mean they are more or less legible and so exclusively fit for use in information design. The design of 'wayfinding' and informational signage requires clarity to function. The relationship of typography and space in these applications can vary considerably from the small signage panel to grand architectural applications. Consistency of style (perhaps of size, too) and the contrast of typography in relation to background will be important in establishing a clear and effective system.

Web

Typography for the web in terms of space and size is usually specified in pixels (px) and em units (em). In recent years, there has been a focus on content strategy (CS) in web development. In this case, the content leads the design, or rather the search for greater clarity and appropriateness of the web experience. This is in contrast to many early web developments in which solely the design and the designer would have had a major influence on what was communicated.

Typography for the web appears more controlled in many instances today too. Much of what is regarded as good typographic practice for print now appears to be migrating to web-page design also. This is in part facilitated by a greater control of how typography behaves on the web, such as through the use of tables, frames, grids and .php dynamic content. Cascading style sheets (CSS) are separately written, coded files that allow for greater control and flexibility of application than do 'in-line tags', which were previously the norm for many web-page HTML source codes. The future of web typography will be enhanced further by the ability to embed fonts within the code and the 'Web Open Font Format' (WOFF) is set to make for a richer typographic web experience.

Ride

Welcome to NewcastleGateshead. This is your free map to help you get around central NewcastleGateshead. Whether you're here for the weekend or just enjoying a day out, this map will help you plan your journey and make the most of your visit.

There is something for everybody to enjoy in NewcastleGateshead. This is just a selection of ideas to ensure an unforgettable visit.

Visit
the BALTIC for the latest contemporary art, explore the Pre-Raphaelites of the Laing Art Gallery, travel back in time at the Discovery Museum or witness the world evolve at the Life Science Centre.

Listen
to a world of music at The Sage Gateshead, sing along to pop and rock at the Metro Radio Arena, relax at a classic concert at the City Hall or hear the biggest international dance DJs at Foundation nightclub.

See
the grand architecture of Grey Street, seek out public artworks around the Quayside and Gateshead Quays, learn about the hidden history of Blackfriars or explore the old halls of the Castle Keep.

Watch
great dramas unfold at the Theatre Royal, the latest performances at the Live Theatre, explore the hippest new dance forms at DanceCity or simply people watch of the Quayside.

Shop
for anything and everything on Eldon Square, buy the latest fashions around Market Street, check out the trendiest street wear on High Bridge or purchase a work of art at The Biscuit Factory.

Meet
amongst the buzz of people at Monument, join friends for a stroll through Leazes Park, come together for the athletics at Gateshead International Stadium or share views from Gateshead Millennium bridge.

Eat
at the many restaurants on the Quayside, spend your lunchtime in the cafés around Grey Street, sample the international menus of Chinatown or enjoy a meal with a view at Gateshead Quays.

Stay
in one of the many hotels in the area – there's something to suit all ages and budgets. That local Visitor Information Centres will be happy to find you a room.

Enjoy
spectacular views of the Tyne's seven bridges, the noisy atmosphere at Newcastle United, revisiting your childhood at Seven Stories in Ouseburn or the lively nightlife of the Bigg Market and The Gate.

Explore

NewcastleGateshead is a fascinating place to explore on foot and has an excellent public transport system to help you get around.

QuayLink electric buses connect all the major attractions and destinations in central NewcastleGateshead. The Metro connects you to the airport, the coast and surrounding areas – both services are fast, frequent and efficient. Use the maps below to plan your journey or visit a Nexus Travelshop for further travel information.

Bus
Buses run to all parts of NewcastleGateshead and the region.

Bus stops are located throughout the area and most routes begin, end or run via one of the central bus stations. In general, buses to the North run from Haymarket Bus Station, to the West from Eldon Square Bus Station, to the East from Market Street/Granger Street and to the South from Newcastle Central Station and Gateshead Interchange (including frequent connections to the MetroCentre).

For connections to other cities, National Express operates from the Coach Station.

Taxi
Black Cab Taxis (Hackney Carriages) can be picked up from major transport interchanges and designated Taxi Ranks. Taxis displaying an Ambassador sticker are trained to provide visitor information.

Taxi journeys between central NewcastleGateshead and Newcastle International Airport take 20–30 minutes.

Train
Newcastle Central Station is a major hub for both national and regional services. The local rail network connects Central Station to destinations throughout the North East.

Cycleways & footpaths
Hadrian's Way and Keelman's Way are long distance cycleways and footpaths that form part of the National Cycle Network and follow the north and south banks of the River Tyne linked via Gateshead Millennium Bridge.

Bicycles can be rented from Tyne Bridge Bike Hire, located within the Guildhall.

Tours
The City Sightseeing open top bus tours start and finish at Newcastle Central Station. Buses run from March to December.

There are two River Tyne cruises: Tyne Leisure Line starting from the Quayside; and Shields Ferry starting from South Shields ferry landing.

QuayLink electric buses

QuayLink electric buses offer a high frequency, accessible and easy to use service. Routes connect the attractions and sights of Quayside and Gateshead Quays with Newcastle Central Station, Haymarket Bus Station and Gateshead Interchange.

Look out for the bright yellow buses running approximately every 10 minutes, 7am to midnight, 7 days a week.

Tickets can be bought on board. All Network Traveltickets are valid.

QuayLink bus stops are indicated by yellow icons on the Walk map on reverse.

Metro
Tyne and Wear Metro is a light rail system connecting all major destinations in the region. Services link central NewcastleGateshead with the airport in 20 minutes, and the coast in 30 minutes. The ride between Newcastle Central Station and Gateshead Interchange takes less than 5 minutes. The Metro is also the ideal way to get to main shopping areas around Haymarket and Monument and the hotels, cafés and restaurants of Jesmond.

Metro trains run daily from 5.30am to midnight, every 5–10 minutes during the day and 10–20 minutes in the evenings. Tickets can be bought from machines at all Metro stations. If you're planning to make several journeys, buy a Metro DaySaver offering a day's unlimited travel.

Park and Ride allows easy access via the Metro to central areas. Park and Ride car parks are indicated on the Metro map.

Ask

Transport information
For all local travel information, visit a Nexus Travelshop located within Metro Stations at Newcastle Central Station, Haymarket, Monument or Gateshead Interchange.

City Sightseeing	07776 203 897
Tyne Bridge Bike Hire	0191 277 2441
National Rail Enquiries	08457 48 49 50
Newcastle City Walking Tours	0191 277 8000
Newcastle International Airport	0870 122 1488
Nexus	0191 203 3333
Shopmobility (Gateshead)	0191 477 9888
Shopmobility (Newcastle)	0191 261 6176
Tyne Leisure Line	0191 296 6740
South Shields Ferry Cruises	0101 203 2215

traveline
public transport info
0870 608 2608

Visitor information
Visitor Information Centres are located on Granger Street next to Central Arcade, at Guildhall on the Quayside and in the Gateshead Visitor Centre, Gateshead Quays.

Visitor information enquiries
Gateshead	0191 478 4222
Newcastle	0191 277 8000

www.visitNewcastleGateshead.com

This map is printed on Elemental Chlorine Free (ECF) pulp obtained from sustainable forests. Please reuse, recycle or pass it on to a friend.

This map is produced by Newcastle City Council with the support of Gateshead Council, NewcastleGateshead Initiative, Nexus and the Tyne/Wear Partnership.

© Newcastle City Council

NewcastleGateshead
world-class culture

Above
In Cartlidge Levene's information panels for visitors to NewcastleGateshead, a strong, clear, functional hierarchy is employed in the design.

Design considerations

There are many aspects to a design problem that need to be taken into consideration when thinking about how type should be arranged on a page. This will depend on what kind of artefact it is that you are designing. Type arrangement for a book will differ to that of a poster, for example. What does the content need to communicate? Who is the readership or intended audience? Ask yourself: do I understand the content? Can I make sense of what needs to be communicated?

There are certain formal considerations that may help you to develop the design scheme. For example, should the design look traditional, modern or postmodern? Should it be symmetric or asymmetric? Will a grid system be used? Identifying an approach may be one way of making decisions about such arrangements. However, it may be that you need to produce a completely unique response to the design problem. Typographic design is not a question of appropriating style. It must serve in communicating *meaning*.

Other considerations may relate to the size and format of the page or the sheet that you are working to. How do the elements of your design occupy the given space? What is the balance or relationship between the elements employed within your design? Have you thought about leaving white space within the design? Should your design create a feeling of tension or harmony? Should the design appear precise and accurate? Does it need to feel less formal? Is it designed to appeal to the quiet and genteel, or does it need to be loud and aggressive?

Whatever your approach, some research and experimentation in terms of the formal elements of type will help you to develop your thinking about the overall design scheme to be employed.

The relationship between display type and text type may be your main concern if you are designing a poster. However, if you are designing a book, you may need to work out exactly what the relationship between page size and text area may be. This will include making decisions about margin sizes, running heads and folios (page numbers), and their position. If your artefact will contain a large amount of text, this will obviously strongly influence any choices or decisions that you make with regard to the design.

Opposite
The handling of text and image in this broadsheet created by Why Not Associates appears playful and effortless, belying the skill and confidence deployed in this complex composition.

Centred typography

Centred typography and compositions may give your design a 'traditional' or 'stable' appearance and in many applications this can work beautifully. For example, traditional centred book title pages, when designed well, still command an air of authority and majesty in their appearance.

However, some truly terrible examples of centred typographic layout can be found in everyday ephemera. This is usually produced not so much by the design, but from a perspective of the 'quaint' or 'nostalgic' adopted by those willing to let the default options of page layout software (or worse still!) word-processing software dictate the appearance of the work.

'Design is always creative because it must always determine its own proportion of values in relation to each other in each part of the design, and to its fitness for the purpose of the design.'

John Charles Tarr
How to Plan Print (1938).

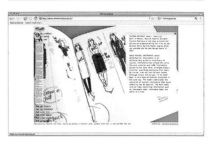

If lines of type are set too long or too short, it can either become difficult for the reader to locate the next line in a paragraph (particularly when there is extended reading matter to consider), or the text can appear broken and interrupted. The setting should take into account letter-spacing, word-spacing and inter-linear spacing (leading).

Ranged left

If lines of type are set too long or too short, it can either become difficult for the reader to locate the next line in a paragraph (particularly when there is extended reading matter to consider), or the text can appear broken and interrupted. The setting should take into account letter-spacing, word-spacing and inter-linear spacing (leading).

Justified, last line ranged left. Indent – one em equivalent

If lines of type are set too long or too short, it can either become difficult for the reader to locate the next line in a paragraph (particularly when there is extended reading matter to consider), or the text can appear broken and interrupted. The setting should take into account letter-spacing, word-spacing and inter-linear spacing (leading).

Ranged right

If lines of type are set too long or too short, it can either become difficult for the reader to locate the next line in a paragraph (particularly when there is extended reading matter to consider), or the text can appear broken and interrupted. The setting should take into account letter-spacing, word-spacing and inter-linear spacing (leading).

Centred

This is not to say that you can't create good design within word-processing software, just that it is the design that should be thought through, not which buttons will give the desired look. With centred typography, especial care needs to be taken over how lines of type are grouped into paragraphs too, as there is no clear edge for the eye to return to when reading from one line to the next. This can occasionally cause problems with readability, as well as producing some rather interesting – if not outright strange – paragraph shapes.

Asymmetric typography

Asymmetric typography, in contrast to centred typography, could crudely be described as having an 'off-centred' appearance, though in practice, there is more to it. Asymmetric typography can crucially create tension and hierarchical order within a composition.

The influence of early twentieth-century pioneers of art and design, such as El Lissitzky, Laszló Moholy Nagy and Kurt Schwitters, and associated movements and groups such as dada, Vorticism, Futurism, De Stijl and the Bauhaus, all helped to produce a new critical, avant-garde approach to typography. This modern or 'new' typography became more refined and in 1928, Jan Tschichold published his manifesto of modern typography *Die Neue Typographie* ('The New Typography'). Tschichold argued for a design for modern times typified by clarity and order; and typography that introduced a clear hierarchy and signposting to allow for greater efficiency in reading and communication.

Modern typography later developed into the Swiss typography of the 1950–60s, which came to be known as 'International Style'. In terms of layout, much of this typography makes use of white space within the design. Grid systems are also a strong feature within modern typography, and were developed further than the modular grids discussed previously. Radial, axial and diagonal compositions developed. Counterpoint, hanging line, attraction or conflict between grouped elements, harmony, pattern, repetition, movement, rotation and rest were all methodological approaches to composition that found their way into typography from the practitioners and teachers of the modern movement.

Opposite top
Mwmcreative's website allows the viewer to rearrange the type matter in relation to the page composition.

Opposite bottom
Some standard paragraph arrangements are displayed here. Note how the bottom two paragraphs do not allow for a fixed position for the eye to return to on the left-hand side.

Opposite
This lorem ipsum exercise is an homage to Jan Tschichold's *Die Neue Typography*. Even though we may not be able to read the text, Tschichold's principles regarding organizing, creating hierarchy and visual signposting within the typographic arrangement are clearly evident.

Just as modernists challenged the traditionalists, so modern typography became challenged through design work that set to ask questions of working practice. Designers like Wolfgang Weingart and Gert Dumbar were among those who helped inspire a generation of younger designers in the 1980s and 1990s to explore and challenge graphic design and typographic conventions. Texts were deconstructed and readings made simultaneous, layered, rich, complex and challenging for their readers.

The impact of computers

The historic changes occurring in graphic design were partly influenced by the introduction of the personal computer. The Mac allowed designers to become their own typesetters and 'authors' of design. Expression, randomness and the arbitrary became a justified approach to design for many.

The freedom of the computer and the exploration of emerging digital media seemed to offer endless possibilities to what could potentially constitute design. For some, these possibilities came close to the point of nihilistic implosion and claims of the pending end of print and the death of the book seemed to point to a bleak future for design and typography.

Typographic approaches today

More recently, there has been a return to the exploration of more formalized and structured approaches to typographic design by many. A far more pragmatic and open view to design has developed. How well does the work communicate? Is it appropriate? Is it ethically sound? These questions may take us a long way from thoughts of layout and arrangement but at least they allow for openness in terms of approach. It is actually fine to mix symmetry and asymmetry as long as there are justifiable reasons for doing so. In short, there are no rules; it is more of a case of practising to find out what works, how it works and why it works.

NEW LOREM-IPSUM

Im IPICA VOLORIBUS AUT QUIDENDITI OMNIS explit qui im aliquisim, restrum qui berum ut ad explit, aliquuntem a non perum:

NEW LOREM IPSUM

Aut excea doluptaqui occum istrum fuga. Nam, es porernat pel magnisi

THE NEW LOREM IPSUM

Doluptam aut aute odi dition nulpa
Tatenda perspel endandis sapitatum dolorem eicae

Doluptam aut aute odi dition nulpa simet esequis nonem il is magniss inieni tem aplenducl tem harlam lam sit et unt volore diorroviti ut moloria aliquun tiossim olorem laboris antum acearum nullorpos velest, sa ipisti ducit, se cusa consequate porendi **STEMPER IONSEQUAM** nistectorem ipisti quamus ent et quias renimus.

Tatenda perspel endandis sapitatum dolorem eicae. Aximpe lautatquam facere porestorera dolecta dolupta pro velique eicatent optaquation ni dia cus, qui illent optaspe rlaersp elluptam qui aliquam quosani miligen ectoreh entiatem quas eost **milicta temporepro dolecatia** senimin nonsequo milis sim aped quo occaepudit as eost, omnis moluptatet es quo voluptate eatiurest que nonempel maximaio escim qui as voluptam ad qui odis coresto ressuntium quasitaquam eicimagnatur a sunt ommos eos **estiae volupta** sapid earum exped mo et es doluptae dolesequi delectem quasperum enlhicl umquatio quias vel entorum is aut odit ipistionem excesto dolorem **ium qui aborese earum** rae dit officatis et laci ne vendam exere simpore reped magnis nisinve lenimporumet qulaspl **tatquod ipsapedis** mod mo doluptas estibus conseque pro torit etusape rspellantia qui sequo offic tecatquat dolo int idendebit placcusa Genihicius inctatem delibus antota et quunt liquiam idendebit placcusa etus aliquae **neculpa seque porae dolorescit** intis que quo officienet di temqui vel et exerspe liquia doluptur, corem vento odicides et erovit es eribus esequunt por rem aceped mo ommoluptas mil iumquibus.

Apide aut exped quat veniam, aut pra inum ad maion culparchit est endione mporias et que pe volupta dolecto que comniet hilitiunt minctem aceatet maionsentio. Optaturit, sunt pa dent abo. Ut reratestiae re nustio. **Oribusam, conestorum velictem** ressinvero et aspis audi nis earumquat vendae quam dolo tem ipsum accum simporerum qui de ventibus eosam quam, omnihic iditam sedipsa evenihi llorers pedigenis a volupti busdae eiur alibus rest, odi ratis iuntin pero officat atibusa ndelici psantio nsequi volorunt, venectur, tempe si as es evel is eos eicil molorrumquos velestio.

Ehendipidis mos et, ipsum anit ratusaest eati dolupis et ommolum id quam ipsam **remquatibus dolupita nimet hicit** qui ute nest magnihictur asit, ventur aligeni hilliti aepero omniet facerem num aborest eatem hit ndelici psantio nsequi volorunt, venectur, tempe si as es evel is eos eicil molorrumquos velestio.

NEW LOREM IPSUM

Qui vel endisciene quatum ut aliquo
Is mo cones ulpa et, simus.
Fic temquatio.
voluptat di
cum il eius eum con resero ditiur?
Qui vel endisciene quatum ut ut.
Taliquo quae. Itatus dolorent, ut antur,

Qui vel endisciene quatum ut aliquo
quatibernati que
delendit et quatiuntiae
asped quas maiore
quos qui dio volupta
simpore ctemod ut
fugia des adis sequatibus.
quatibernati que
delendit et quatiuntiae
asped quas maiore
quos qui dio volupta
simpore ctemod ut
fugia des adis sequatibus.
Tur? Qui ut qui
eperovit, eostoremquae
qui doluptate vellita e
praectium aut
vendae non cus.
Tem nos in conse
placepr ovitia viduciliquo

Qui vel endisciene aliquo
nonsequiam aut aut ero et quo qui
est, con

Apide aut exped **125** veniam, in op inum ad maion culparchit est endione mporias et que pe **200** dolecto que hilitiunt minctem aceatet maionsentio. Optaturit, sunt pa dent abo. Ut reratestiae re nustio. Orionagi.

Tatenda perspel endandis sapitatum   **2.00**
Tatenda perspel endandis sapitatum   **3.00**

Opposite
The numerical
representational forms
within the logotype
for 'Cent Quatre' are
explored in relation
to the event date
in this identity and
poster jacket by
Experimental Jetset.

Below
In this playful cover
by Paulus M. Dreibholz,
the content of the text
is explored through
the form of the type
composition.

Type only

Typography in its purest form – that is to say, without supporting photography and illustration – can be equally challenging and highly rewarding to produce when the outcome works successfully. Earlier in this book, Beatrice Warde's famous 'Crystal Goblet' speech was discussed. Warde argued that typography should be invisible in order to allow content to be communicated. In many instances, this is still a sound argument, even so many years later. However, even the simplest of typographic pages creates an overall image. The selection of good quality typefaces will certainly make a huge difference when working with type only. This is true of both 'invisible' typography and of the highly conspicuous sort.

Think about how your type 'speaks' to your audience. Is it timid and shy or quietly humble? Is it proud and confident or loud and annoying? Despite what Beatrice Warde argued, we are either consciously or subconsciously influenced by the form of the type that we read, both in terms of text and display typography.

Type doesn't need to be large and colourful to create an impact. A simple, well-designed book page can create an overall impression or tone, contrary to what has been argued by some. Eric Gill once said that '…letters are things, not pictures of things', meaning that letters are symbols used to represent something: sound. The same is true for all typographic elements, whether they are letters, words, lines, paragraphs or pages. Each of these elements is symbolic, in that they represent something else; be that a single sound (phoneme), a word sound and the concept that this represents, or the meaning of a sentence and so on. They are all representational of how we communicate something of our world.

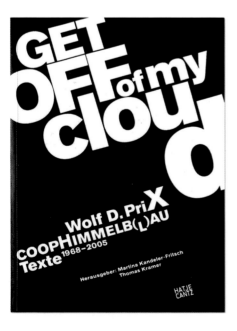

MAIRIE DE PARIS
LE 104 CENT QUATRE
ÉTABLISSEMENT ARTISTIQUE DE LA VILLE DE PARIS
OUVERTURE
11 OCTOBRE 2008
14H30 A 2H
ENTREE LIBRE
104 RUE D'AUBERVILLIERS
5 RUE CURIAL
75019 PARIS
T 01 40 05 51 71
WWW.104.FR
LE 104
CENT
QUATRE
ONZE
OCTOBRE
2008
LES PARTENAIRES DU CENTQUATRE:

Opposite
This Christmas card
by Andrew Haslam
treats the gospel text
of Luke in an almost
scientific analytical
manner, creating an
intriguing information-
design-like image of the
composition.

Below
The scale of New
York City can be felt
in the cropping of the
composition in this
piece by MadeThought
for The Mill.

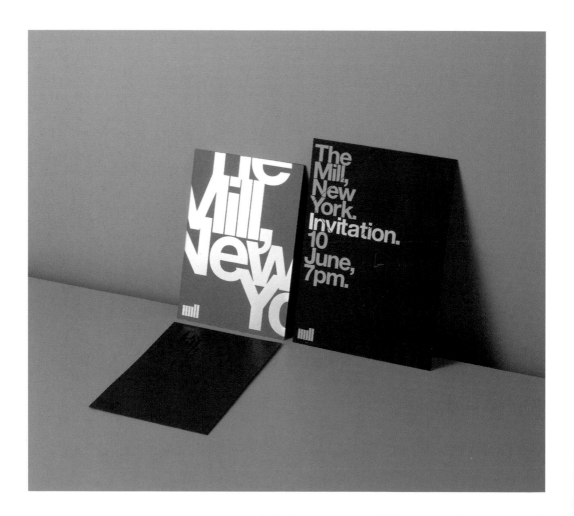

Shape and form

Visualized as typography, all typographic elements or symbols must take on form. Whether it is at the detailed level of a single character, or the complex structure of a highly organized page, the shape and 'feel' of a design will also evoke meaning to some degree. It is not only the content that has meaning; form too is charged with the *potential* of meaning. Attention to the relationship between communicating content and how the form of the typography can facilitate this – either helpfully or not – will help provide interesting and useful solutions when working with type. As with all aspects of design and typography, taking time to critically reflect on what you do is important, too.

Once the overall concept has been developed, attention to detail in work that is exclusively typographic will make a noticeable difference. This is true of both fastidious book work as well as of expressive promotional work. The thing is to have a go! Be creative, be expressive, question, challenge and experiment – this is the only way that you will find out for yourself. Research, read about the formal aspects of typography, test to see how type works at different sizes with different spacing and leading.

Don't ignore the rich history that has gone before. There are many great pieces of work that use type only: study them and ask why they work so well. Practice and experimentation with type will lead to confidence in working with it. And pure type works best when it has been confidently handled.

Combining elements

Combining type and image requires some careful consideration. It is not always as straightforward as you might expect. Like all aspects of graphic and typographic design, how you deal with this will largely depend upon what the design is intended *for*. However, in terms of placement, there are only a few simple variables to consider, as we will explore below.

Images can sit alongside type

This can obviously be in any direction from the type but this is where type and image sit separately from each other. This could be found within the pages of a magazine, newspaper or book, for example, where a whole page or an area of a page contains an image and the corresponding type is set at some distance from this.

Images can sit within the body of the type

This is where type may be set within columns on a grid. Images may be small and occupy just a single column within the type or occupy several column widths. Care has to be taken when images spread across columns that break the visual flow of the reading. When type is set in columns, we read from the top to the bottom of the page and work from left to right across. Images that are the width of the whole number of columns should perhaps be positioned above or below the type if the type represents one continuous story or feature.

Type can appear in front of the image

Type that appears to be placed on top of an image can be quite difficult to handle. There are considerations to make not just regarding how the type will impact on the image itself, but also regarding how placing the type upon an image will affect the legibility and readability of the type. If the type is too small or too light in weight, the image will quite often have the effect of breaking this up. The image may need to be reduced in contrast or to be treated with a monotone colour 'wash' or tint; that is, be given a simple treatment so that it appears to be largely composed of one colour, thereby creating a stronger contrast between type and image.

Opposite
In this example of the author's work, the audience is invited to literally 'look through' the last 100 years in relation to this exhibition poster. The format and elements create their own grid, whilst acknowledging the impact that modernism has had on shaping art and design education during this period.

portsmouth
1908—2008
exhibition and degree show

one hundred years of art and design

Animation Design
Communication Design
Design for Interactive Media
Fashion and Textiles Enterprise
Fine Art
Illustration
Photography
Restoration and Decorative Studies
Three Dimensional and Decorative Design

Access to HE Art, Design and Photography

Portsmouth School of Art,
Design and Media
Eldon Building
Winston Churchill Avenue
Portsmouth PO1 2DJ

Contact:
Melanie Lang
T: +44 (0)2392 84 3801
melanie.lang@port.ac.uk
www.port.ac.uk

Open to the public:
07.06.08–13.06.08
10am–4pm Daily

Show opening:
06.06.08
6pm–9pm

The Fashion Salon:
06.06.08
6pm, 7pm and 8pm

Another way to achieve the effect of type appearing over an image is to have the type appear in boxes or panels that either knock out the image or render it translucent, effectively reducing the contrast of the image behind it.

If of a large enough size, particularly in display sizes, the type may appear translucent itself. This can be adjusted to allow the image to be seen through the type. A similar effect is achieved by overprinting the type onto the image, usually using ink colours that allow the details beneath to be seen.

Overprinting has seen a fashionable resurgence in recent years as a technique used by many; however, its early use arose more out of necessity due to certain limitations in aspects of the printing process rather than through choice. There is an immediacy and authenticity about the appearance of overprinting when well executed.

Opposite
In this spread by Nick Bell for Eye magazine, the qualities of the layered imagery are echoed in the form and composition of the text.

Below
In this cover by Gerard Unger, the image shows through the large typographic elements enabling a simultaneous foreground/background reading of text and image.

Images can appear in front of the type

This may be achieved in much the same way as detailed in the last paragraph in terms of translucency and overprinting. Also, if the type is large enough (as with very large display settings) and the images are small enough, these may be placed upon the type with no real loss of readability.

Images can appear inside the type

This involves basically using the outline of the type as a picture box. If handled well, this can be effective; more often than not, however, this kind of treatment can look very predictable if not executed well.

Type can sit within the image

This effect can be achieved either by setting it up within the photograph itself or by carefully manipulating the image with software. Use of photo-manipulation software is quite often to blame for many crimes against typography – so approach with caution! The software is useful for certain applications as long as you don't get carried away with the array of filters and effects available. Design requires consideration, not automation.

Beyond language alone

Type is form and ultimately form alone. We cannot help but make images with type when we produce our designs. Yet, because we see so much type around us in our day-to-day lives, our understanding of typography is saturated by the deluge of impressions that surround us. In the busy towns and cities that most of us populate, we rarely notice the rich assortment of letterforms and typography that are to be found on the street. We have become less sensitive to the image that a block of text makes or to the patterns formed by paragraphs in relation to a page layout.

However, when we discuss the idea of type as image we are usually referring to type that appears at display sizes. This also means type that often purposefully goes beyond the role of purely communicating language. The term 'type as image' does not refer to making obvious pictures from type either, as in using typeface characters as a kind of mark-making tool – although there are some notable examples of where this has been achieved successfully.

Type as image may explore the sculptural character of letterform. Type sizes may be so greatly enlarged that we begin to see them as taking on new and unique qualities. Characters may be used more abstractly. They may ignore their intended symbolic use as a signifier of sound and appear to form new relationships and bonds with other type characters and symbols and so create new meaning or explore purely visual qualities.

Hendrik Nicolaas Werkman

Hendrik Nicolaas Werkman (H. N. Werkman) was an artist and printer born in 1882 in the Dutch province of Groningen.

He is regarded as one of the pioneers of the discovery of expressive display typography or type as image in the early twentieth century.

In 1920, Werkman became a member of the Dutch artists' group 'De Ploeg' (The Plough) for which he printed notable promotional material. However, he became increasingly interested in adopting an avant-garde approach to his work, experimenting with type in an expressive, almost paintorly manner. He produced work by the combined use of typeface, printing blocks, stencilling and stamping. He also developed methods of printing from found materials that gave his work unique and exciting qualities. Amongst his methods were Tiksels, Druksels and Hot Printings.

In 1940, shortly after the German invasion of Holland, Werkman set to work printing and publishing a series of Hasidic stories under the name of 'De Blauwe Schuit' (The Blue Barge). These were intended to act as a subtly rebellious commentary on the Nazi occupation occurring at that time. Werkman was arrested by the Germans in March 1945 – three days before the liberation of Groningen. He was executed along with nine others by a Gestapo firing squad. The H. N. Werkman College in Groningen now bears his name in memory of the advances he made in design.

Opposite
In this letterpress piece by Phil Baines, the word 'omega' takes on greater visual significance with the aid of a backdrop of celebratory form and colour.

Above
In this student experimental type project, the functioning of the heart valves and flow of oxygenated blood is explored in a sequence of purely abstracted typographical compositions.

Below
The combination of modular type and composition in this poster by Hamish Muir/ 8vo demonstrates how type can function as image as well as text.

Opposite
MadeThought's 'Unfold Japan' poster creates a playful type/image relationship from the content and form of the type used.

Experimenting with type

Many of the early pioneers of modern typography explored the nature of type as image. Typography was allowed to break free from its formal, restraining, metal-letterpress straightjacket. Type would be printed directly onto the page by hand, it would be collaged, it might appear within montages.

Type became expressive and dynamic. It would create tension and be used to explore the structure of language itself in relation to its visual appearance. Type compositions became abstracted, even painterly.

Type was used to explore the possibilities of composition. In this form, type was also used to create political statements.

Experimenting with type can be a great way to get to know type better. It can be fun and expressive. It can also give greater insights into how letterforms behave when they appear at very large sizes, for example.

Many of the formal considerations of arranging and setting type may need to be suspended. When constructing type as image, anything goes – the creative parameters are left completely open to the imagination. It does still require practice, however.

This form of typography may abandon many of the formal considerations of other aspects of typographic practice, but sensitivity and an eye for detail are still important factors that need to be adopted. And, above all, taste and appropriateness still prevail.

Clarity and order

Hierarchy in typography helps to create clarity and order for the reader. Many older conventions or etiquette governing typographic hierarchies have given way to those developed from modern typography.

Hierarchy helps to provide clear visual signposting between different ordered elements within a design. Hierarchy may be achieved through the ordered use of any of the following elements within a design:

headings
subheadings
stand-firsts
text type
captions
running heads
folios
pull quotes or display quotes
marginal or footnotes

It is the designer's job to make sure that the information to be communicated is understood appropriately. One of the ways to achieve this is to work out if the information content will break down into more manageable and easily identifiable chunks. If this is the case, then the designer can specify the visual relationships and levels of order that should exist between these different sections of content.

Hierarchy is also about creating enough discernible contrast between distinct elements – but not so much that they end up fighting against each other.

It is usually a good idea to begin with what will come to form the text type. For example, if you were designing a brochure that you decided needed a clean, modern look and feel, you might choose Akzidenz Grotesk Light 8/10pt (8pt type on 10pt leading) for the text type. The subheadings need not be any bigger in size, but might appear in the bold weight of the same font.

You may decide to have a line space between the subhead and the text, although this can sometimes make subheads appear to float from the text. If the subheads are to appear larger, then this need be no more than a 2pt increase in size. Headings for your brochure may appear much larger if necessary, as these would be considered display type; however, a sense of proportion and the relationship of the headings to the text size would need to be carefully judged.

The relationship between type sizes and weights is also important. These may appear as only slight differences at first, but they can make a huge difference to the overall design.

Above
Art directed with bespoke fonts by A2 Design, a clear and thorough hierarchy can be seen in this book about the British artists Jane and Louise Wilson.

Right
This spread by Paulus M. Dreibholz shows how typographic hierarchy also helps to build structure in the layout. It is clear, clean and architectural, befitting the subject matter.

Seeing and reading

Two words that have great significance in relation to typography that you will hear mentioned very often are 'legibility' and 'readability'. Legibility and readability as terms are also quite often mistaken to mean the same thing in relation to typography.

'Legibility' refers to how clear or well defined something appears. This often refers to type at the single character level or the word level. It relates to certain qualities that are characteristic of typefaces. A font can be considered more or less legible, or illegible, based upon how clearly it appears when set at different sizes. Printing processes, inks, colours and materials are also factors that can affect how clear, identifiable or legible typography may appear.

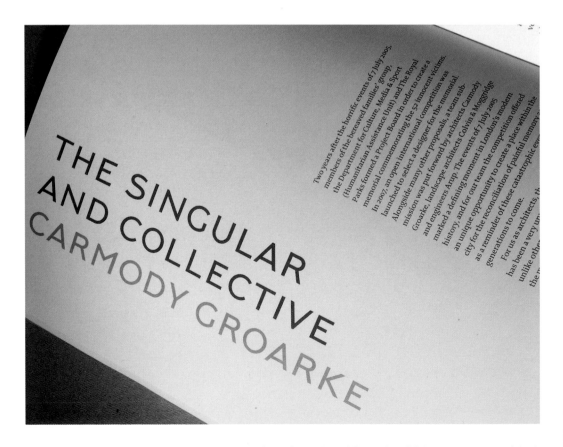

Opposite
The text and display
setting in this business
portfolio designed
by Phil Baines and
Catherine Dixon
shows great clarity
and restraint, thereby
creating a very legible
and readable text.

Right
Cartlidge Levene's
typography for Carlisle
Group here uses a bold
sans serif as a text type,
but still maintains a
perfectly legible and
readable text-matter.

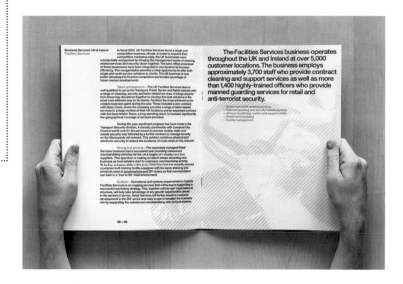

'Readability', as the word suggests,
refers to how readable typography
may be. Some of the factors that can
make typography illegible will also
have an effect on how readable it will
be. Again, the choice of type, quality
of printing, colour, materials and so on
are just some of the things that may
have an effect on this. The size of the
type, line length, leading, spacing and
the alignment of type may also have an
impact on readability.

If you are working with typography,
it is worth bearing in mind that the
main job of type is for it to be read by
someone else. Becoming familiar with
and choosing good quality typefaces,
using and practising with these in
different settings, and seeing for
yourself where problems of readability
or legibility may occur by adjusting the
size, spacing and leading of type are all
aspects that designers should look to
fully develop in their work.

'To achieve harmony and legibility is the main
object of typography.'

Oliver Simon
Introduction to Typography (1945)

Typographic colour

The term 'typographic colour' is used in design to refer to the overall quality or texture that a text setting may have. Typographers may state that they prefer text that has an evenness or greyness of colour. This is achieved by paying attention to the micro-details of typography and to the impact this has upon the overall appearance of the type.

The choice of typeface will be a determining factor as to whether a good or even colour can be achieved in the typesetting. Again, use of good quality, well-drawn types are important. The kind of typeface will also have an effect. Whether this is serif or sans serif will count; different kinds of serif and sans serifs will create further effects again. Choosing a typeface is almost like selecting a type of thread to weave into material. This tiny detail of the decision-making process will have a significant impact on the quality and feel of the finished product.

Letter spacing, word spacing and line spacing (leading) all change the look of a text dramatically too, so this needs to be sympathetically approached. Lower-case letter spacing is usually frowned upon, but small adjustments may be necessary. Too much and words break apart; too little and they become cluttered and look like blots on the page. Word spacing needs to be handled with care. If it is too wide, then 'holes' will appear within the text. If it is too little, words will appear to run into each other. Similarly, if line spacing is too narrow, the text will look thick and heavy; if it is too wide, lines will begin to separate.

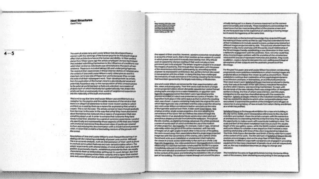

Above
The evenness of typographic colour is evident in this book spread from A2 Design.

Opposite
Type and spacing choices contribute to typographic colour. This also impacts on the readability of text. Top paragraph: the spacing is at normal setting. Middle: there is too much letter, word and line spacing here. Bottom: this shows the same paragraph with too little spacing.

If lines of type are set too long or too short, it can either become difficult for the reader to locate the next line in a paragraph (particularly when there is extended reading matter to consider), or the text can appear broken and interrupted. The setting should take into account letter-spacing, word-spacing and inter-linear spacing (leading). Each of these elements will have an influence not just on the overall appearance of the text, but also on how the text functions. It is important to recognise that text typography and display typography require different levels of attention to detail also. This is not to say that similar issues will not apply in each case. It may be however, that certain details become more or less apparent depending upon the application of the type.

If lines of type are set too long or too short, it can either become difficult for the reader to locate the next line in a paragraph (particularly when there is extended reading matter to consider), or the text can appear broken and interrupted. The setting should take into account letter-spacing, word-spacing and inter-linear spacing (leading). Each of these elements will have an influence not just on the overall appearance of the text, but also on how the text functions. It is important to recognise that text typography and display typography require different levels of attention to detail also. This is not to say that similar issues will not apply in each case. It may be however, that certain details become more or less apparent depending upon the application of the type.

If lines of type are set too long or too short, it can either become difficult for the reader to locate the next line in a paragraph (particularly when there is extended reading matter to consider), or the text can appear broken and interrupted. The setting should take into account letter-spacing, word-spacing and inter-linear spacing (leading). Each of these elements will have an influence not just on the overall appearance of the text, but also on how the text functions. It is important to recognise that text typography and display typography require different levels of attention to detail also. This is not to say that similar issues will not apply in each case. It may be however, that certain details become more or less apparent depending upon the application of the type.

Type and colour

Colour choice is a very important consideration for type matter, particularly for text type, where the effects will be noticed more readily. The choice of colour employed for typographic matter may have an impact on factors such as legibility and readability of the type. In the majority of cases, text typography will probably appear as black type on a white background. However, the use of a white that is not bright white, but rather a natural or off-white is usually preferred, especially in book typography.

It is the contrast between type-matter and background that is affected when different colours are used. Too high a contrast and type can appear to dazzle or flicker; too low a contrast and the type will disappear.

Certain colours for text type should be avoided also. Yellow type on a white background will appear invisible as will white type reversed out from yellow. Yellow has the effect of appearing to spread, so it makes it difficult to discern the edges of the type.

For this to work, the type size would need to be set at large sizes, or the yellow would need to be mixed with a small amount of another colour so that it would appear to have more weight.

Similarly, certain reds can be problematic to read also. Combinations such as blue and green, light blue and orange, red and green should also be treated with care. Some colour combinations are not only difficult to read but may appear invisible to readers with some forms of colour blindness.

Finally, take the advice provided by Josef Müller-Brockmann, that working with limited colour palettes can actually prove beneficial when it comes to design. Simple one- and two-colour jobs can force us to think more creatively about the colours that we choose and how we might best apply these. After some practise, you will begin to discover for yourself what combinations work best.

'The sparing, but methodical and logical use of colour has a more telling effect than a combination of many different colours. If colour is used, it should be plainly visible and the reasons for its use immediately apparent.'

Josef Müller-Brockmann
The Graphic Artist and his Design Problems (1961)

Sam que rehenit atemperio corem everum ut alisim fugiatur? Dolupis el is non pore dignihitis ea inullabo. Neque iligeni ditate num que pe etur sinvello experibus ad unt alit eum re omnisque.

Sam que rehenit atemperio corem everum ut alisim fugiatur? Dolupis el is non pore dignihitis ea inullabo. Neque iligeni ditate num que pe etur sinvello experibus ad unt alit eum re omnisque.

Sam que rehenit atemperio corem everum ut alisim fugiatur? Dolupis el is non pore dignihitis ea inullabo. Neque iligeni ditate num que pe etur sinvello experibus ad unt alit eum re omnisque.

Sam que rehenit atemperio corem everum ut alisim fugiatur? Dolupis el is non pore dignihitis ea inullabo. Neque iligeni ditate num que pe etur sinvello experibus ad unt alit eum re omnisque.

Sam que rehenit atemperio corem everum ut alisim fugiatur? Dolupis el is non pore dignihitis ea inullabo. Neque iligeni ditate num que pe etur sinvello experibus ad unt alit eum re omnisque.

Sam que rehenit atemperio corem everum ut alisim fugiatur? Dolupis el is non pore dignihitis ea inullabo. Neque iligeni ditate num que pe etur sinvello experibus ad unt alit eum re omnisque.

Sam que rehenit atemperio corem everum ut alisim fugiatur? Dolupis el is non pore dignihitis ea inullabo. Neque iligeni ditate num que pe etur sinvello experibus ad unt alit eum re omnisque.

Sam que rehenit atemperio corem everum ut alisim fugiatur? Dolupis el is non pore dignihitis ea inullabo. Neque iligeni ditate num que pe etur sinvello experibus ad unt alit eum re omnisque.

Above
Colour affects both readability and legibility. Black on off-white is regarded as being one of the most legible combinations. However, it is wise to test any ideas that you may have about using colour before committing these to your design. Some combinations are best to avoid.

Creating a simple poster

This task is about putting things that have been discussed so far together into one design.

Task 3

Create an A2 (420 × 594mm) poster from your own working definition of typography. Write a short 100-word description of typography which explores your knowledge of the subject so far.

Give your description a title. For example, this might be: 'Typography is…'. Once you have written your account and have a title, design a grid system for your A2 page. Draw this onto A2 paper (computer not permitted), then decide whether you will use a simple column type grid or a modular one. Decide what width the columns and margins should be.

Using one simple sans serif font (for example, Gill Sans, Helvetica or your preferred choice) typeset your copy onto the computer to 10pt type with 12pt leading in size, making sure that this is set to the width of one of your columns. Set your title in the same font (this can be a bolder weight) at different sizes, ranging from say 48–100pt. Print these out. Photocopy the text and title to various sizes of enlargement, then cut these out.

Using the grid as your guide, arrange your text and title to form as many design compositions as you can within one hour. Then photograph them with your camera or mobile phone.

Use these photos as a record of what worked best afterwards. Recreate your best example on the computer, making notes of measurements and distances from your cut-and-pasted original.

The only rule to bear in mind is that the text type must work as text type should. That means that this must be clear, readable and legible in the end. Your display typography can be anything from ordered and sophisticated to loud and aggressive!

Tip

Try to have a plan of what you aim to explore in the layout. For example, a difference in scale and proportion, tension, balance or symmetry might be possible themes to explore. Try to really push the ideas. Don't be afraid to scale type to huge sizes. Explore the size and format of the page area. Remember: type can crop, exit, rotate, repeat and so on.

NB: The main point of the exercise is to work at 100 per cent scale. Producing a poster on the computer can never been seen at its intended A2 size. We continually zoom in and out when working on the computer and this gives a false impression of the final scale.

Below
Working at the same size as the design can give an overall sense of scale and proportion but may be hard to achieve when working on computers due to restrictions of screen size and the ability to zoom in and out.

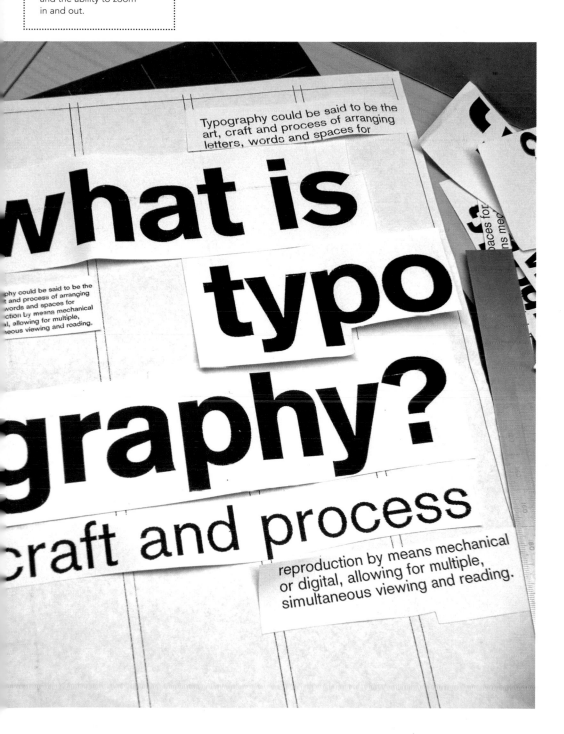

Typography could be said to be the art, craft and process of arranging letters, words and spaces for

what is typo graphy?

craft and process

reproduction by means mechanical or digital, allowing for multiple, simultaneous viewing and reading.

Once you become interested in typography, you will want to know how certain things work. And the more you look, the more you will find. Before you know it, you will notice tiny details in typographic matter that were previously invisible to you. You can't learn all these things at once and quite often there are no quick or easy ways to do so. Keep looking, questioning and practising. You will continue to learn about typography throughout life, and you should be pleased about that!

Attention to the detail of typography will improve your work, but learning typography is like learning to play a musical instrument — you will get better with time and practise. You must also practise regularly. You might learn to play a piece of music very well on one piano but you may not be able to play the same piece equally well on another. The same could be said for working with typefaces and using them in different contexts.

This chapter will look at how you can refine your typographic matter, particularly when dealing with text type. We will explore some of the phenomena and methods related to working with the finer points of typography rather than learning a set of strict rules.

Type size

When you select a type size, this is usually set in points (pt), or sometimes in pixels (px) for screen work. Many designers have adopted working in metric sizes also. It has already been mentioned that when selecting type sizes for text settings this may work best between the sizes of 8–14pt. This will largely depend upon other factors that you must also consider, namely line length or column width, but also context of the design, format and anticipated use or audience. You should bear all these things in mind when making decisions about type size. There are also a few further details peculiar to type that you will need to consider, which we shall explore below.

Type has two sizes – a given size and an appearing size

When you select a type size, you are selecting the size of the body of the type. When a typeface is designed, the letterforms are designed within a space with a given fixed aspect height. This is similar to the metal or wooden body of letterpress type. The space must accommodate the variations in height of all the characters (glyphs) within the font. Ascenders, descenders, punctuation and accents all sit within this space. When you select a type size on the computer, you are specifying that you want this body to appear at the given size. So if you select 10pt, for example, it is the body that appears at 10pt. The type that sits within this body may therefore appear smaller or larger depending on the design and how it occupies the body space. The baseline for most fonts (the general exception may be some display fonts) is common, however.

x-height x-height
x-height x-height

Above
The top line shows both types in the same given point size; you can see how the sans serif appears too large in line with the serif type. The bottom line shows the sans serif reduced in size to optically harmonize with the serif type.

Left
Type size denotes the size of the body just as in lead type. The typeface appears within this body size and will alter in optical size depending on the design.

Adobe Garamond Pro 10/12pt
If lines of type are set too long or too short, it can either become difficult for the
reader to locate the next line in a paragraph (particularly when there is extended
reading matter to consider), or the text can appear broken and interrupted. The
setting should take into account letter-spacing, word-spacing and inter-linear
spacing (leading). Each of these elements will have an influence not just on the
overall appearance of the text, but also on how the text functions. It is important
to recognise that text typography and display typography require different levels
of attention to detail also. This is not to say that similar issues will not apply in
each case. It may be however, that certain details become more or less apparent
depending upon the application of the type.

Apple system Garamond 10/12pt
If lines of type are set too long or too short, it can either become difficult for the
reader to locate the next line in a paragraph (particularly when there is extended
reading matter to consider), or the text can appear broken and interrupted. The
setting should take into account letter-spacing, word-spacing and inter-linear
spacing (leading). Each of these elements will have an influence not just on the
overall appearance of the text, but also on how the text functions. It is important
to recognise that text typography and display typography require different levels
of attention to detail also. This is not to say that similar issues will not apply in
each case. It may be however, that certain details become more or less apparent
depending upon the application of the type.

Stemple Garamond 10/12pt
If lines of type are set too long or too short, it can either become difficult for the
reader to locate the next line in a paragraph (particularly when there is extended
reading matter to consider), or the text can appear broken and interrupted. The
setting should take into account letter-spacing, word-spacing and inter-linear
spacing (leading). Each of these elements will have an influence not just on the
overall appearance of the text, but also on how the text functions. It is important
to recognise that text typography and display typography require different levels
of attention to detail also. This is not to say that similar issues will not apply in
each case. It may be however, that certain details become more or less apparent
depending upon the application of the type.

Opposite
Just because typefaces share the same name does not mean that they will look and behave in the same way. These three interpretations of Garamond show not just how aesthetically different they may be, but also how they perform differently at the same size.

If you were to select a word in 10pt Garamond roman and next to that a word in 10pt Helvetica, you will notice that Helvetica appears much larger. This is to do with the design of the type within the body, so they have the same measurement but appear different in size. If you do use two different typefaces within the same text, these should normally be adjusted to appear the same size visually. A tip here is to look at the x-height for each and adjust this so that it appears as the same height.

A single typeface or font may have different optical sizing or scaling

Many text fonts today have their typeface characters drawn to an optimum 12pt standard. This provides a robust average so that the type can be scaled between text and display settings. Some typefaces have specific optical variations. This allows the type to function more appropriately at smaller and larger sizes. For example, those types intended for use at caption size will usually appear wider and heavier than their 12pt counterparts. Similarly, variations to be used at larger sizes may show a lightening of the strokes and a reduction in the width of serifs.

If you are using a font that includes optically scaled variants, use the one most appropriate to your specification (that is, if working in 10pt, use the nearest 'drawn' size).

'No art demands for its perfection more tenderness than the art of typography.'
Christian Heinrich Kleukens

Leading

Leading is also referred to as line-spacing or interlinear spacing. The term 'leading' derives from metal type where horizontal strips of lead of given point sizes (or depths) were inserted between lines of type to adjust a text's vertical spacing. The adjustment of the spacing was necessary (as it is today) to allow for a visual evenness of the type composition. Today, we specify leading size as well as type size on the computer in points (pt).

As a general guide, and by default within many of today's design software packages, leading for text settings is normally set around 120 per cent of the type size. That is to say, if we select 10pt Garamond within a page layout program, the program will 'auto' set the leading for 12pt. We may then say that we are using Garamond 10 on 12pt or 10/12pt. The leading value is not adding an extra 12pt to our 10pt, however. The way that we might think practically about this is to say that we have a 10pt type on a 12pt body, so in essence we have 10pt type + 2pt leading. We can imagine the 12pt measurement as the distance between baselines in a paragraph of text.

There are a couple of considerations to bear in mind, however. Don't rely on default settings: specify your own. For example, if we had 12pt Garamond, 'auto' setting at 120 per cent would give us 14.4pt leading, which is an irrational figure perhaps best rounded up or down.

Different typefaces will require different amounts of leading so that they appear comfortable and even. Type needs room to work, and some types need more than others. Also, try to avoid over-spacing or under-spacing your lines of type, as this will impact on the readability of the text.

As type increases in size, the relative ratio of leading to type size may have to be reduced. This is particularly noticeable at display sizes. So type at 100pt will appear to have far too much space between lines if the leading is 120pt. This needs to be adjusted to work visually. At very large sizes, leading values may often need to be smaller than the type size, depending on the application being used.

If lines of type are set too long or too short, it can either become difficult for the reader to locate the next line in a paragraph (particularly when there is extended reading matter to consider), or the text can appear broken and interrupted. The setting should take into account letter-spacing, word-spacing and inter-linear spacing (leading). Each of these elements will have an influence not just on the overall appearance of the text, but also on how the text functions.
10.5 / 13pt

If lines of type are set too long or too short, it can either become difficult for the reader to locate the next line in a paragraph (particularly when there is extended reading matter to consider), or the text can appear broken and interrupted. The setting should take into account letter-spacing, word-spacing and inter-linear spacing (leading). Each of these elements will have an influence not just on the overall appearance of the text, but also on how the text functions.
10.5 / 15pt

Above
Creating too much or too little space between lines interrupts the act of reading. Top: shown here is an acceptable degree of spacing between lines. Bottom: the lines here have become separated and appear less like a coherent paragraph.

Line length

Along with the choice and size of typeface, letter-spacing and word-spacing, line length is a very important consideration for the typographic design. The length of the line of type will indicate the width of the type area or column width; this is also referred to as the 'measure'. It is important that lines are neither too long nor too short, as this will affect the readability of the text. A line length of between 50 and 70 characters wide is a useful guide to providing a good line length. This will provide an average of around 8 to 12 words per line in the English language.

The average word length in English is approximately the length of five characters, so add a character to this to allow for word-space and you can work out the average words per line.

For example:

$5 + 1 = 6$
(average word length in English)

$50 \div 6 = 8.333$
(round this down to 8)

$70 \div 6 = 11.666$
(round this up to 12)

This serves as a guide only. For some publications, such as magazines, brochures, technical manuals and dictionaries, the line length may be less. Other publications may require longer lines to be set.

What kind of design it is that you are producing will also need taking into account. Line length can get us to read at different speeds, which is useful to know when considering the content of the material that you are working with. Shorter lines can allow us to read more quickly – useful for newspapers and magazines where we want to digest information at a quicker pace. Longer lines, by contrast, can help to slow down the reading speed. This is useful for book work, for example, where it may be necessary for the reader to take their time in digesting the content.

If lines of type are set too long or too short, it can either become difficult for the reader to locate the next line in a paragraph (particularly when there is extended reading ...
approx 60 characters per-line – comfortable line length

If lines of type are set too long or too short, it can either become difficult for the reader to locate the next line in a paragraph (particularly when there is extended reading ...
approx 30 characters per-line
too short for comfortable reading

Top
The number of paragraphs per line helps us to pace our reading.

Bottom
Shorter lines make us read more quickly. But if they are too short they will destroy the flow of reading.

Kerning

The term 'kern' was originally given to a part of a typeface character that by nature of its design overhung the type body, usually encroaching on the body of a neighbouring character when set. This was sometimes necessary for certain characters so that the space between these elements would appear visually correct when printed.

Sometimes, the space between letters requires adjusting to compensate for odd spacing that might appear as a result of certain letter combinations. It is this individual adjustment of space between letters that is now referred to as 'kerning'. Most awkward combinations are taken care of by the type designer, but there are occasions when you will need to make manual adjustments between letters.

The need to kern letters may become more apparent as type increases in size and this is particularly noticeable in display settings. In many cases, the eye has to play the role of judge, although certain software programs will allow you to give values for 'kerning pairs'. Here, the designer can specify which characters need kerning and to what extent, and can apply these changes globally to a text or job.

As a general rule, rounded letters (C, O, c, e, o, and so on) and angular letters (A, V, W, Y, v, w, y, and so on) require slightly less or reduced space around them. Characters with a strong vertical emphasis (H, I, l, i , and so on) will need more space than rounded characters. Others include certain upper- and lower-case combinations (Av, Ay, Ta, To, Va, Vo, Wa, Wo, Ya, Yo and so on). The lowercase 'f' can also sometimes cause problems; however, most fonts include at least 'fi' and 'fl' ligatures (special combined characters) for these instances. These should be used in text but may often not work so well in display, so care needs to be exercised. In terms of numerals, the spacing of the number 1 (one) often needs to be adjusted.

Punctuation may also require an adjustment of space if this to sit comfortably with the text. Upper-case only settings need to be kerned and / or tracked – the larger counter spaces within the characters require the space that surrounds them to be increased (the leading too if set over more than one line).

Below
Although the letters here appear evenly spaced, the blue squares show that mathematically, the vertical characters require more space between them than the rounded or diagonal characters in order to appear visually correct to the eye.

Hill

Hoover

'Ninety per cent of the proofs which disappoint the typographer owe their failure to please to an utter disregard of spacing…'

Vincent Steer
Printing Design and Layout

Tracking

In addition to kerning, type settings may also require tracking applied. Tracking values can be set to increase or decrease the overall spacing values of a setting. This can be done for many reasons. Perhaps the particular choice of typeface set at a certain size appears to have letter and word spacing that is too large or small. Tracking can be increased or decreased to adjust and compensate for this in order to improve readability.

Also, as was briefly mentioned earlier, if a text setting is in upper case only, then this will require overall additional spacing. When set together, upper case letters must be allowed to 'breathe'. Because of their more regular appearance in terms of height and width, internal spaces – counters and so on – appear larger; therefore, the surrounding space must be adjusted to compensate for the visual 'holes' that may appear in these kind of settings. The internal and external spaces of these letters when composed need careful attention.

Tracking can also be useful when space is at a premium in text settings; a small 'minus tracking' applied to a text may save valuable space within a job. Applied to text across the pages of a book, this may even reduce the number of pages required or free up additional space for pictures and illustrations. In newspaper or magazine settings, where narrow columns are used, tracking can help to 'ease' an additional word per line.

In general, tracking should be used to make small adjustments to text. Too much additional tracking and words will break apart, too much minus tracking and letters and words will begin to bunch up thereby causing the text to appear spotty or patchy.

Below
Care needs to be taken if applying tracking to text settings, as this may have a detrimental effect on the reading. Only very small amounts should be considered (for example, +3 or –3). Here, zero tracking is most acceptable. Your rule of thumb should be: if in doubt, do not track text.

If lines of type are set too long or too short, it can either become difficult for the reader to locate the next line in

minus 25 units tracking

If lines of type are set too long or too short, it can either become difficult for the reader to locate the next line in

zero tracking

If lines of type are set too long or too short, it can either become difficult for the reader to locate the next line in

25 units tracking

If lines of type are set too long or too short, it can either become difficult for the reader to locate the next line in

50 units tracking

Spacing

The spacing of text takes on three forms: letter-spacing, word-spacing and line-spacing. We have already looked at line-spacing or leading and mentioned that leading must be carefully considered depending upon the choice of typeface, the type size and the line length.

Letter and word-spacing are also important. This is perhaps difficult to see at first when you begin to work with type, but with practice the eye is trained to spot the smallest of details.

Letter-spacing should not be altered without due reason. That is to say, if you don't know *why* you are altering it, then don't do it. However, when needed, letter-spacing can be altered by adjustments to tracking values within some software programs or by setting justification values.

Letter-spacing should not be too closely set as this will result in letters crashing together. Where letter-spacing is too close in bodies of texts, letters may clump together causing distracting and unsightly patches within the text. This should be avoided. Likewise, if letter-spacing is increased too much, words will break up and the spaces between letters and words may no longer be discernible. Bolder or heavier types may require a slight narrowing of letter-spacing compared to lighter types, particularly when the type size is increased.

The word space is determined by the design of the chosen type in use. It is designed to work as part of the font. Again, this may appear to work perfectly well at text sizes, so there may be no need to change this. However, as a guide, the word space should appear to be equivalent to the width of the lower case 'i'. The word space traditionally had width values relative to the 'body' size or 'em' in lead type. Em, en, thick and thin spaces are available in some fonts and software programs still today.

Below
As a guide, the width of the lower case 'i' provides a good measure for word-spacing. This may need to be reduced as type size increases, for example in display type settings.

Both word-spacing and letter-spacing will again require adjustment to appear optically correct as type size increases and in display settings. This usually requires a small reduction in the spacing. Bolder or heavier types may require a slight narrowing of word-spacing when compared to lighter types.

Word-spacing can be adjusted within justification settings where available in software programs. Alternative spaces – for example, em and en – can be inserted via the keyboard or glyph palettes and contextual menus where applicable. Additional spaces for special settings may include three-per-em, four-per-em and six-per-em spaces.

words should be spaced evenly

word spacing and type size

word spacing and type size
word spacing and type size

'It should be a rule that lowercase is never and under no circumstances to be letterspaced.'

Jan Tschichold
On Typography (1952)

H&Js

Adjustments that have been mentioned in terms of letter-, word- and line-spacing are sometimes referred to as 'justification'. Designers often refer to this in connection with 'hyphenation'. 'H&Js', or hyphenation and justification, refers to the control of adjustments over a body of text and how these will behave given certain numerical values or parameters.

For example, we can detail that we want our text to appear without hyphens at the end of a line of text. Instead of words being split, they are then pushed over to the next line of type. Many typographic designers prefer to set type 'ranged left' without hyphenation. This is a particularly purest approach to type because it leaves words unbroken. It also means that the edges of paragraphs may appear more aesthetically pleasing because there is no visual disturbance from hyphens, which tend to attract the eye.

In many cases, however, we may need to include hyphenation. If this is the case, it is best to make these settings so that no more than two hyphens will appear on consecutive lines of type.

Letter-spacing and word-spacing can also be set to minimum, optimum and maximum values. Take care that these are not set to extremes, as small adjustments will have a big impact on the overall look and texture of the body of type.

Finally, the width of the letters themselves can be adjusted; though this is usually frowned upon by many designers. However, tiny adjustments of around 1–3 per cent are permissible. This will be virtually imperceptible also, but may prove to be very useful especially when dealing with long texts or narrow columns where space may be tight. A tiny adjustment of this nature can help to make the copy fit.

If lines of type are set too long or too short, it can either become difficult for the reader to locate the next line in a paragraph (particularly when there is extended reading matter to consider), or the text can appear broken and interrupted. The setting should take into account letter-spacing, word-spacing and inter-linear spacing (leading). Each of these elements will have an influence not just on the overall appearance of the text, but also on how the text functions.
H&J word space 'opt' 100%

If lines of type are set too long or too short, it can either become difficult for the reader to locate the next line in a paragraph (particularly when there is extended reading matter to consider), or the text can appear broken and interrupted. The setting should take into account letter-spacing, word-spacing and inter-linear spacing (leading). Each of these elements will have an influence not just on the overall appearance of the text, but also on how the text functions.
H&J word space 'opt' 85%

If lines of type are set too long or too short, it can either become difficult for the reader to locate the next line in a paragraph (particularly when there is extended reading matter to consider), or the text can appear broken and interrupted. The setting should take into account letter spacing, word-spacing and inter-linear spacing (leading). Each of these elements will have an influence not just on the overall appearance of the text, but also on how the text functions.
H&J word space 'opt' 75%

If lines of type are set too long or too short, it can either become difficult for the reader to locate the next line in a paragraph (particularly when there is extended reading matter to consider), or the text can appear broken and interrupted. The setting should take into account letter-spacing, word-spacing and inter-linear spacing (leading). Each of these elements will have an influence not just on the overall appearance of the text, but also on how the text functions.
H&J word space 'opt' 100% and letter space 0%

If lines of type are set too long or too short, it can either become difficult for the reader to locate the next line in a paragraph (particularly when there is extended reading matter to consider), or the text can appear broken and interrupted. The setting should take into account letter-spacing, word-spacing and inter-linear spacing (leading). Each of these elements will have an influence not just on the overall appearance of the text, but also on how the text functions.
H&J word space 'opt' 85% and letter space 'opt' -2%

Above
Getting to know how hyphenation and justification settings work is very useful for fine-tuning type. This can help to improve readability in text setting, as well as managing the amount of space the type occupies.

Traditional type spacing
Spacing in lead type was based around division of the 'body' or em of the type. This comprised:

Em quadrant (or 'mutton' quad)
= the body

En quadrant (or 'nut' quad)
= half of the body

3-em (or 'thick' space)
= one third of the body

4-em (or 'middle' space)
= quarter of the body

5-em (or 'thin' space)
= one fifth of the body

Hair space
= approximately one twelfth of the body

Special characters

Beyond the standard layout of the keyboard, you will find that producing typographic work may require you to use accents on characters or to use punctuation and symbols that you have previously been unfamiliar with. These 'special characters' may be contained within a standard font. For use in Western Latin-based languages, these have a basic set of 256 characters. Most people are unaware of or have not often used many of these characters. Each key is assigned a special 'Unicode' number. You may notice that there are slight differences between keyboard layouts for Mac and Windows systems, although some fonts can be shared by these platforms. It is the Unicode assignment that the font responds to.

Creating accented characters may be achieved by typing combinations of 'alt' + accent key followed by the character.

Some examples are:

¨ (alt + u) + u = ü

The same follows for other characters: ä, ë, ï, ö, ÿ.

´ (alt + e) + e = é

The same follows for other characters: á, í, ó, ú.

^ (alt + i) + i = î etc.

Special accents and characters may also be accessed via a glyph palette found within some software programs; this allows these additional 'special characters' to be placed within the text by means of a 'point and click'.

A standard font typed on a Mac keyboard includes:

Standard: §1234567890-= qwertyuiop[]asdfghjkl;'\`zxcvbnm,./

+ shift: ±!@£$%^&*()_+QWERTYUIOP{}ASDFGHJKL:"|~ZXCVBNM<>?

+ alt: ¡€#¢∞§¶•ªº–≠œ∑´®†¥¨^øπ"'åß∂ƒ©˙∆˚¬…æ«˙Ω≈ç√∫~µ≤≥÷

+ shift & alt: ⁄™‹›ﬁﬂ‡°·'—±Œ„‰ÂÊÁËÈØ∏""'ÅÍÎÏÓÔÒÚÆ»ŸÛÙÇ◊ı˜¯¿

Right
Shown here is a specimen of Jeremy Tankard's Enigma, showing roman, italic and small caps, as well as the Eszett ligature (the German double 's'), and accents or diacritical marks.

Bottom
Some typefaces may also include decorative special characters, such as swashes. The example shown here is from Tankard's Aspect typeface.

Memorable

Vă rog arătați-mi pe hartă

Straße

FURNISHED ROOMS

çarşı

Ik ben de weg kwijt

swash swash
& & & &

Expert (and OpenType Pro) fonts

In addition to special characters to be found within the standard font set, additional sets of characters are available that may be required for complex settings or for when something unusual or sophisticated is called for.

In terms of digital fonts, these extended sets were available (and still are today where they exist) as an 'expert set'. These were separate but related to the standard set. A typical expert set would probably contain a full set of ligatures (ff, fi, ffi, fl, ffl), old-style figures (non-lining numerals), small caps and sometimes fractions and additional non-standard ligatures, mathematical symbols or ornaments.

Although these additional characters are very useful to a designer, they can sometimes be difficult to work with in practice. This is especially true when dealing with large documents. It was (or still is in many cases) a lengthy 'find and replace' exercise or a job of working back over the original text and highlighting and replacing.

Today, 'OpenType Pro' format fonts can make things much easier for the user. The type designer can programme into the font attributes that can be switched on and off by the typographer or graphic designer within the design and layout program. Switching on particular attributes saves the long 'search and replace' procedure required with separate expert sets.

Like all aspects of typographic design, however, working with 'OpenType' fonts requires a certain degree of restraint to be exercised. Not all jobs will require large sets of ligatures, for example; but for special occasions, this might be just what is called for.

biðstöð

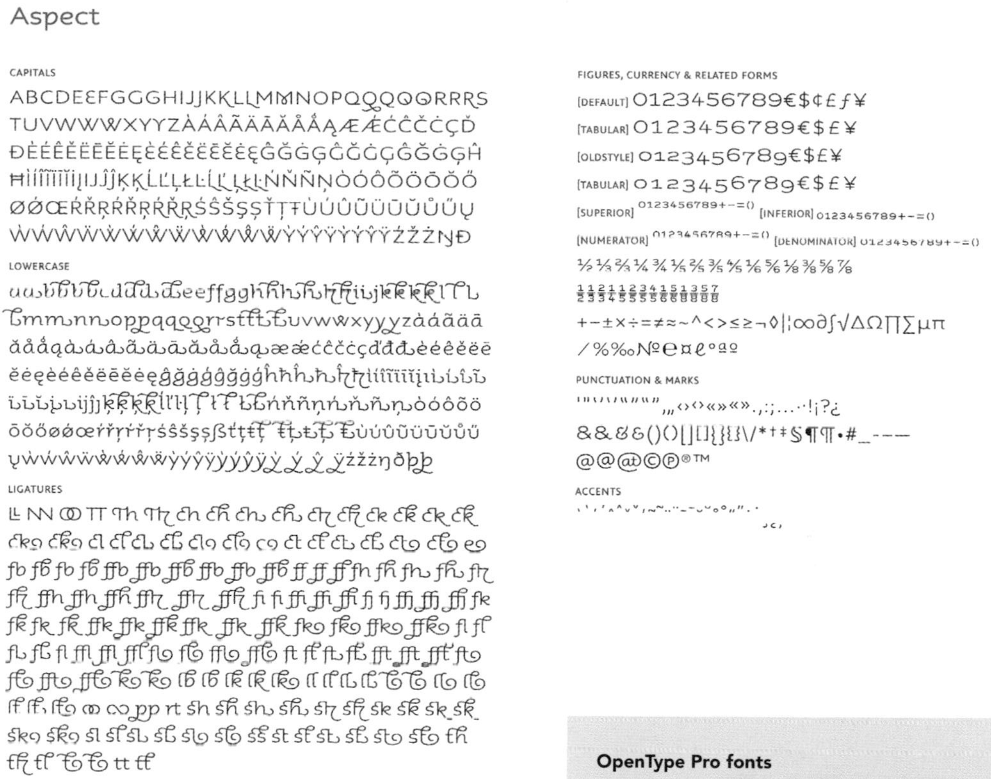

Aspect

CAPITALS

ABCDEƐFGGGHIJJKKLLMMNOPQQQQQRRRS
TUVWWWXYYZÀÁÂÃÄĂĀÅÅĄÆÆĆĊČĈÇĐ
ĐÈÉÊËĚĖĒĘÈÉÊËĚĖĒĘĜĞĠĢĜĞĠĢĜĞĠĢĤ
ĦIÍÎÏĨĬĪJIJĴĴĶĶĹĽĿŁĽĹĽŁĿŁŃÑŇŅŃÑŇŅÒÓÔÕÖŌŎ
ØŐŒŔŘŖŔŘŖŔŘŖŚŜŠŞŚŢŤÙÚÛÜŨŬŪŮŰŮÙ
WWŴŴŴŴŴWWWWWYÝŶŸYÝŶŸŹŻŽŽŅĐ

LOWERCASE

ɑɑʊɓɓʋɓċɑ́ɑ̃ɑ̃ʤeeffgghĥĥɦ̃ħ̃ɦiiʲjk̇k̇ķķ̨ḷłĿ
ɭmmₙₙₒoppqqₒrrsfffʦʦʊvwwxyyyzàáâãä
ǎɑ̊ɑ̊ɑ̨ɑ̊ɑ̊ɑ̊ɑ̊ɑ̊ɑ̊ɑ̊ɑ̊æǽĉċčçďɑ̄ɑ̄ɑ̨èéêë
ěęėєe̊e̊ē̊ēe̊ęĝǵġģĝǵġ ĝǵ ĝĥĥ ĥ̃ ħ ħ̃ iíîïĩĭïiïĭĭ ùúûüũ ũ
ùùḷ̊ꞵ̊ijĵĵķķ̨ķ̨ꞁꞁꞁꞁ ꞁ ʦ̊ ꞁ̊ ŀ ñ ñ ñ ñ ñ ñ ñₙ ₙ óòôö
ōŏøœŕřṛŗśŝ šşßçţťṭ ꞇ̃ꞇꞇʦ ùúûüũŭ ũ ũ
ꞵwwŵŵŵŵŵŵ yýŷÿyýŷÿyýŷÿ ý ẏ ẏ żźžž ŋ ðþþ

LIGATURES

LL NN ꝏ TT Th ꞇꞧ ch ĉh ĉh ĉh ĉꞧ ĉꞧ ĉk ĉk ĉk ĉꞧ
ĉk-ꞧ ĉk-ꞧ ꞇl ꞇl ꞇl ꞇl ꞇl ꞇl-ꞧ ꞇl ꞇl ꞇl ꞇl-ꞧ eꞧ
fb fb fb fb ffb ffb ffb ffb ffb ff ff ffh fh fh fh
ffi ffh ffh ffh ffh ffi ffi fi fi fi ffi ffi fj ffj ffj ffj fk
fk fk fk ffk ffk ffk fk ffk fk ffk ffk fl fl
fl ffl ffl ffl ffl ffl fꞇo fꞇo ffꞇo ft ff fꞇ fꞇ fft fft fft fft
fꞇo fꞇo ffꞇo ꞇo ꞇo lb lb lk lk lk ll ll ll ll ꞇo ꞇo lo lo
lf lf lfo ꝏ ꝏ pp rt ꞩh ꞩh ꞩh ꞩh ꞩꞧ ꞩꞧ ꞩk ꞩk ꞩk ꞩꞧ
ꞩk-ꞧ ꞩk-ꞧ ꞩl ꞩl-ꞧl ꞩl ꞩlo ꞩlo ꞩꞩ ꞩt ꞩl-ꞇl ꞩl ꞩlo ꞩlo fꞧ
ffꞧ ꞇl ꞇo ꞇo tt ff

FIGURES, CURRENCY & RELATED FORMS

[DEFAULT] 0123456789€$¢£ƒ¥
[TABULAR] 0123456789€$£¥
[OLDSTYLE] 0123456789€$£¥
[TABULAR] 0123456789€$£¥
[SUPERIOR] 0123456789+-=()   [INFERIOR] 0123456789+-=()
[NUMERATOR] 0123456789+-=()   [DENOMINATOR] 0123456789+-=()
½ ⅓ ¾ ¼ ¾ ⅓ ⅔ ⅜ ⅝ ⅛ ⅝ ⅜ ⅞ ⅞
$\frac{1}{2}\frac{1}{3}\frac{2}{1}\frac{1}{2}\frac{3}{2}\frac{1}{3}\frac{2}{5}\frac{3}{5}\frac{1}{8}\frac{3}{5}\frac{7}{8}$
+−±×÷=≠≈~^<>≤≥¬◊¦¦∞∫√ΔΩΠΣμπ
∕%‰№℮№ℓ°ªº

PUNCTUATION & MARKS

'''"'""""‚„‹›«»‹‹››.,;:…·!¡?¿
&&&&()()[][]{}{}|\/*†‡§¶•.#_‐‐—
@@@©®™

ACCENTS

`´ˆˇ˘¯¨˙˚˝ˉ~¸˛ºⁿ‚„'"·
˒˓

Opposite
Here, Enigma shows
the old English or
Icelandic 'eth' character.

Above
Jeremy Tankard's
Aspect shows the
range of characters and
alternates included in
this 'Pro' font.

OpenType Pro fonts

OpenType Pro fonts are primarily based
on the structure of TrueType fonts but
with the addition of 'smartfont' features.
These enhance and extend the use of
and user interaction with the font.
OpenType Pro fonts can have TrueType
or PostScript outlines or 'flavours'.

When compared to the previous font
standard 256 character set, OpenType
fonts can have up to 65,536 characters.
This allows any language categories
under the Unicode system to be
supported.

For languages such as English, which has
a simpler character base, OpenType fonts
can contain many augmented features
and functions.

These fonts are also intended to be
cross-platform, meaning that they can
be used by both Mac and Windows
operating systems.

Spaced out

This task gets you to look at the small stuff: the spaces within and between letters, the spaces between words and the spaces between lines.

Task 4

Using the 100-word definition of typography that you created for task three, create a text box within a page layout program and place the text within the box. Set the width of the box to 85mm wide and make sure that there is sufficient depth to the box so that all of the text can be seen.

Change the font to Garamond 10pt with 10pt leading and make sure that this is ranged left (align left). This can usually be done with the type palette or measurements bar within page layout programs.

Duplicate the whole box and place these side by side with 10mm between them. Change the leading in the second box to 12pt. Repeat this twice more, increasing the leading 2pts each time. You will now have four boxes of text with varying amounts of leading. Make a note of which setting appears to read more evenly.

You can repeat this procedure and make changes to word spacing within the program's 'justification' settings.

Once you have done this, do the same with the letter spacing.

Note each time which values give better or more comfortable reading matter.

Try this also with different fonts. This may not seem like the most exciting task to perform as a designer, but it is one that will give you insight and confidence when handling text type if practised regularly.

Tip

Take your time and look at the small changes. It is these that will have a big impact on any large body of text.

Small adjustments
have a big impact
on continuous text
settings. Practising
and experimenting
with these is a useful
exercise. It is also
something that you
will eventually need
to do if you work with
lots of text matter in
your designs.

Using the 100 word definition of typography you created for task three, create a text box within a page layout program and place the text with the box. Set the width of the box to 85mm wide and make sure there is enough depth to the box so that all of the text can be seen.

Change the font to Garamond 10pt with 10pt leading and make sure this is ranged left (Align left). This can usually be done with the type palette or measurements bar within page layout programs.

10/10pt

Using the 100 word definition of typography you created for task three, create a text box within a page layout program and place the text with the box. Set the width of the box to 85mm wide and make sure there is enough depth to the box so that all of the text can be seen.

Change the font to Garamond 10pt with 10pt leading and make sure this is ranged left (Align left). This can usually be done with the type palette or measurements bar within page layout programs.

10/12pt

Using the 100 word definition of typography you created for task three, create a text box within a page layout program and place the text with the box. Set the width of the box to 85mm wide and make sure there is enough depth to the box so that all of the text can be seen.

Change the font to Garamond 10pt with 10pt leading and make sure this is ranged left (Align left). This can usually be done with the type palette or measurements bar within page layout programs.

10/14pt

Using the 100 word definition of typography you created for task three, create a text box within a page layout program and place the text with the box. Set the width of the box to 85mm wide and make sure there is enough depth to the box so that all of the text can be seen.

Change the font to Garamond 10pt with 10pt leading and make sure this is ranged left (Align left). This can usually be done with the type palette or measurements bar within page layout programs.

10/16pt

Choosing fonts

It has been mentioned that fonts need to be chosen for their intended purpose and use. Decide whether you need a text typeface or display type. Remember, text types may also work for display. However, there are thousands of individual display types that can be selected and your decision on this matter will ultimately be one of style and appropriateness.

Text types, on the other hand, need to function in a very different way. Think about what the work is intended for; a text type traditionally intended for a book setting may look too formal or fussy for a magazine, for example. Is the typeface readable and legible at small sizes?

In order to develop some appreciation of text types, it may be wise to begin with some of the classics; for example, Bembo, Caslon, Garamond, Bell, Ehrhardt, Baskerville, Plantin, Bodoni and Scotch Roman may provide a good starting point before moving onto more modern text alternatives. Above all, go for quality. Choose text types from reputable and established foundries and designers. Free downloads from the Internet are rarely up to the job of setting type for extended readings.

Mixing fonts

If you are thinking about mixing fonts, stop! Ask yourself what your reasons for doing this are. If you can, keep it simple: stick to a single font family and create hierarchy with the variants roman, italic and bold and so on.

If you need to use a second font, make sure that it is one that creates a contrast with the first. Don't mix two serif fonts or two sans serif fonts together; there usually won't be enough distinction between them and so it will more than likely look like a mistake in your work. Mix one serif and one sans serif font together, for example. Only in the most complex settings should you need to use more than two fonts together.

You may find 'super' font families that contain a range of serif, sans and slab serif members. These may prove useful for balancing a contrast of variants whilst complementing each other harmoniously. There may be occasions, however, especially with regard to display typography, where a cacophony or riot of fonts works very well, given enough thought as to the reasons for using them.

Communicating with fonts

As well as the function of different kinds of typefaces, fonts also add voice, character and tone to a piece of work. Even if you try very hard to make your work appear as neutral as possible, the fonts that you choose will still be communicating something – neutrality. This in itself is very subjective anyway. To some, Helvetica may be cool and modern: to others it is dull and boring; it can also be precise and scientific, or affected and highly stylized. It really depends on the context of the work and how the viewer sees it.

Have a reason for choosing a particular font. What should it communicate to the audience? Also be careful not to go too far with things. Don't overstate the point, as this can look obvious and clichéd. Choose appropriately. You wouldn't expect to see a solicitor's letterhead set in Comic Sans MS (although no doubt one exists); likewise a 'fun day' for children may not give quite the right message if the promotional material used the formal, elegant ITC Galliard.

Each typeface has semiotic properties, which we usually describe adjectivally: a 'warm' font, a 'strong' font, a 'stoic' font and so on. Try to think beyond personal taste only. Your choice of font will say something about you as a designer. It will also say something about a client to an audience. Make sure that you are communicating appropriately and are not just being carried away by the latest trend.

CHARLEMAGNE

Cooper Black

ENGRAVERS MT

Eurostyle

Impact

Marker Felt

Modern no. 20

PERPETUA TITLING

Playbill

STENCIL

TRAJAN PRO

Wide Latin

Above
Some common system display fonts are pictured here, showing a variety of 'voices'. Note the difference in how diverse the range of type styles are compared to the text types on page 75.

Sizing fonts

Have a rationale for the sizing of your type. Start with the text type and work out the various sizes in relation to this. For example, if you are making a distinction between text and subheadings, there often doesn't need to be a change in size. Using a contrast of variants (for example, roman and bold) is usually enough to make these distinctions.

If a change in size *is* needed, make this a 2pt increase for the subhead; this usually gives enough contrast without looking overly 'heavy'. There is also enough difference in size for the change in size not to look like a mistake. There is often no need to increase both the size and the weight, so test this out too. If mixing serif and sans on the same line, size these so that the x-heights are equal. Remember, as you increase the size of fonts you will also need to pay attention to the spacing. Display sizes, in particular, may need letter and word-spaces reduced.

Default typography

When producing typographic work on the computer, don't just rely on defaults. As a designer, you should be making the decisions about paper size, margins, grids, columns, choice of font, type size, leading, line length and colour yourself. Many of these are set as defaults but won't be appropriate for your own work. Test and make your own decisions.

Defaults can be useful to begin with for things like H&J settings. If you're not sure of how to use these, leave them until you have time to experiment; as your work becomes more refined, you will need to know how these microtypography defaults should be adjusted too. Do not use forced bold, italic, outline, underline and strikethrough. Find the correct font for the job first and check whether the software 'buttons' replace with the correct 'font family' variant.

Alignment

If possible, left align your text. This allows for even word spacing. It also gives the eye a clear edge to return to when reading longer texts. Some designers prefer not to, but if you need to, hyphenate the line endings. Make sure that you have no more than two hyphens on lines next to each other. Justified settings create an even left and right edge to the text, but word and letter spacing needs attention as this expands and contracts to allow the text to fill the space. This can cause problem 'holes' and 'rivers' in text. This kind of alignment is often used in book settings where it can work well.

Right alignment can be useful for captions and small amounts of text, but is difficult to read in longer settings as there is no fixed point for the eye to return to when reading. Centred alignment should be used with care; this has no fixed right or left edge, so can be tiring to read in longer texts.

Detailing paragraphs

When setting paragraphs, don't mix alignments. Stick to one system. Pay attention to line length. This can be shorter for texts intended for quicker readings, like newspapers or magazines. Lines should be made longer for text where we may take our time reading, or for lengthy texts, such as books. Make decisions as to whether to include hyphenation in the text. If you left align, be careful of hanging words at the ends of lines; small words in particular may need to be taken over to the next line.

As well as keeping to a system for alignment, do the same for paragraph breaks. Start new paragraphs with a line space (or half-line space) between. Alternatively, begin new paragraphs with an indent. Don't mix the two. A standard size for indents should be that of the em of the type in use. That is to say, if using 12pt text type, use a 12pt indent. The first paragraph in a section or chapter should not be indented.

Drop caps may be used at the start of a chapter or section, but care should be taken with these. Too many can become repetitious and tedious. You also need to be careful that consecutive drop caps on a spread do not spell embarrassing words, as these will be noticed at a glance. As a guide, drop caps should ideally occupy the depth of three lines of type.

If possible, use a baseline grid when working with paragraphs in multiple columns. You should even out or 'cross align' these, making sure that baselines align from column to column.

Watch out for 'widows' and 'orphans'. The former is a short word on a line of its own at the end of a paragraph; the latter a word on its own line at the top of a new column. These are both undesirable and should be avoided.

E puditiandae q
bus aut et exp
mint essuntiae
lecum remqui sed ul
blaut dusam quos de
ent porita quodion s
Eptis accusciis verur
anditi rehent volupt

Left
Shown here is an example of a three-line drop cap.

Tracking and scaling

As has been mentioned before, there are times when you will need to track the spacing of type depending upon the setting and also the nature of the typeface itself. Tracking should be used sparingly in text settings, but it may be necessary to do this to improve readability at times, or may be desirable if space is at a premium. Tracking should not be altered so that it has a detrimental effect on the grouping of letters to form words. Lower-case type should rarely be given additional space between characters.

Larger type sizes will require some adjustment of tracking and kerning, as spacing become more apparent the bigger the type gets. Also, heavier weight types, for example bold and black, may need the spacing reduced between characters in order to balance the space within the counters of the letters.

As a rule, do not horizontally scale type. This tends to distort the features of the typeface. If you force the expanding or contracting of a typeface, don't. Find a type that does the job. The exception here may be very small adjustments plus or minus, between one–three per cent for text type if additional space is required, or if this helps to improve the readability of the type in relation to the letter and word spacing. Very minor adjustments are acceptable, although some designers may refuse to do this also.

Setting conventions

There are many detailed setting conventions for typography and it is beyond the scope of this book to list them all. However, some common examples are given below to use in everyday typographic settings. This is an area that you will also need to develop as particular issues of setting arise. Care should always be taken with the spacing around punctuation, as this often needs to be kerned, especially at larger sizes where problems appear more obvious.

Abbreviations

In modern usage, abbreviations do not always require a full point:

Prof M Smith, Dr D Brown, etc.

Where a full point is used, however, the single word space that follows should be reduced:

Prof. M. Smith, Dr. D. Brown, etc.

Acronyms

These are words made from the initial letters of organizations' and companies' names. They may be treated with an initial cap only, or as all caps. If treated as all caps, this is often made small caps in text settings. Full points are not normally applied.

Riba or RIBA, not R.I.B.A.

Ampersand

The ampersand (&) is an abbreviation for 'and'; it is derived from the Latin *et*.

In text, the word 'and' should be spelled out. The ampersand symbol may be used in display or to make associations, also in company names and so on.

Smith & Brown, *not* Smith and Brown.

Apostrophe

An apostrophe denotes a possessive association or is used to abbreviate certain words:

Dr Brown's diary isn't on the desk.

Care should be taken with some usage:

It's funny that its bookmark is still there.

Brackets (parentheses)

Brackets should be set without a word space separating content. However, where possible, spacing should be eased with kerning or with font metrics.

(Typography) *not* (Typography), [Typography] *not* [Typography] etc.

Capitals (initial letters)

Initial capitals should be used for names and so on.

Dr D Brown's School of Medicine

But are *not* necessary for headings or titles such as:

Dr D Brown
How to take your medicine and like it.

Dashes

Two forms of dashes are mainly used within text:

En dash – and the em dash —

These should not be confused with the hyphen -

In text, the en dash should have a word space each side. When separating numerals, there is no space:

Dr David Brown invites you – and you alone – to the opening tonight.

Be there between 6–8pm.

The em dash is sometimes used in book settings, where a larger pause in the dense reading matter may be desirable. This appears without a space either side. The em dash should not be used to separate numerals.

Dr David Brown invites you—and you alone—to the opening tonight.

Dashes may require some adjustment in terms of baseline shift when used in small-caps settings and with non-lining figures.

Dates

British style is set thus:

16 January 2011

US style:

January 16th, 2011

Ellipses

Used to denote omissions. Sometimes referred to as a three-dot leader.

If representing the missing part of a word, these should not be preceded by a space:

His last words were 'the diary is on the d…'

Spaces either side are used when denoting a missing word:

Dr Brown left the … he returned some time later.

Fractions

Where possible, specially designed fractions should be used that complement the font. However, these can be made by using 'superior' and 'inferior' numerals set with the 'virgule' (fraction diagonal). The solidus (the standard slash) should not be used:

$\frac{2}{3}$ not 2/3

Hyphens

Hyphens should only be used to join broken or compound words:

Happy-go-lucky, day-to-day and so on.

A hyphen should not be confused with a dash and should not be used in place of this.

Ligatures

Ligatures are specially drawn glyphs that replace some awkward character combinations. The most common are:

fi and fl, sometimes ffi and ffl may be included in a standard font.

These are intended primarily for text, as at display sizes, the spacing may appear odd.

Special sets of ligatures may be available in 'Pro' fonts, but the use of too many ligatures within a text will give a strange appearance. A text may look peppered with these if care is not taken.

Measurements and maths symbols

Set measurement units and symbols thus:

10×10 cm = 1 m

Word spacing may need to be kerned slightly between elements. NB: use the multiplication sign and not the lowercase x. Use correct mathematical symbols wherever possible.

Numerals

Two main sorts of numerals exist: 'lining' and 'non-lining' (old-style) figures.

1234567890 1234567890

Lining figures should be used in tabular work and in caps-only settings (the number 1 in lining figures may need spacing either side adjusting when not used in tables).

Non-lining figures should be used in upper- and lower-case text setting where possible, as 'lining' figures tend to look too large at times.

NB: Some fonts may also include additional small caps numerals.

Point – full, decimal and mid

A full point (period or full stop) is used to end a sentence. In typographic work, this should be followed by a single word space only, not two as in some forms of typing convention.

A decimal point or mid point should be used for monetary work. In financial lists and tables, this may need aligning on the point:

£224·50

100·25

7·30

98·76

The mid point can sometimes look awkward when used with non-lining figures and small caps. It may be necessary to adjust with a slight baseline shift. Some authors and editors may insist on the full point being used, however.

Prime

Primes ' and " are often referred to as 'feet' and 'inch' marks but should not be used for apostrophes or quotation marks. Italic versions of these may be used instead of roman to soften their appearance in settings.

Annoyingly for some typographers, these are referred to as 'apostrophe' and 'quotation mark' in some glyph palettes.

Quotes

Quotation marks may appear differently depending upon the language setting.

British setting is for the use of single quotes. If quoting within a quote, double quote marks are used inside single quotes:

'Yes, then he told me "it's on the desk" before he passed out', she whispered.

Punctuation appears outside the quote but inside if a complete sentence. The full point should not be placed outside if the quote is a complete sentence in itself or if it ends a sentence containing the quote.

'Yes, then he told me "it's on the desk" before he passed out.'

American quotation is often a reversed form of the British:

"Yes, then he told me 'it's on the desk' before he passed out," she whispered.

Note the punctuation inside quotes in American setting.

French language setting may use:

‹ Yes, then he told me « it's on the desk » before he passed out. › (This can also be case sensitive).

In German:

„Yes, then he told me ‚it's on the desk' before he passed out."

And in Spanish:

‚Yes, then he told me „it's on the desk" before he passed out.'

NB: It is often desirable to 'hang' quotes just outside of the text area where these would otherwise interrupt the alignment of a paragraph.

Registered and Trade Mark

The Register mark ® should appear at text size as shown and not made superscript as thus ®.

The trademark ™ symbol should appear as in this line.

Care with spacing and kerning may need to be observed also.

Small caps

Small caps may be used within text for acronyms, company names and abbreviations:

The BBC is based in the UK.

It may also be used where capitalization may look too large and distracting:

Black Oil Farm
Slippery Road
Oilhampton
OLI IOL
UK

Some prefer to set postcodes on the county line also:

Black Oil Farm
Slippery Road
Oilhampton OLI IOL

Care should be taken to ensure clarity, however.

Small caps may be used when setting characters' names within plays also:

DR BROWN He told me before he passed out.

PROF SMITH But was the diary on the desk?

Underlining

Underlining for type should not be used if at all possible. This is a convention normally used by authors and editors to indicate text that is to be set or converted into italic. Underlining disturbs the descenders of the text and interferes with readability:

Peggy gaped, jumped up and wiggled her nose.

Emphasis should be made using a font variant such as italic or bold. If it is necessary to underline, set a rule under rather than underscore the text.

The correct use for underlining is when indicating a hyperlink:

www.underline.com

Typography as an activity has always been synonymous with technology. The word 'typography' itself refers to technology in the form of 'type', the early cast metal bodies upon which the typeface was the surface that the image of the letter was printed from. So it is no different today that knowledge of typography must also include some knowledge of technology.

It is possible to make typographic work in a lo-tech way. That is not in question. However, the reality is that if you are to become skilled in the design and execution of typographic matter, you will need to understand how this is practically achieved. Most advertised design jobs will require knowledge of the appropriate and latest software packages. As a student of design, you will become aware that there is no substitution for great concepts and ideas. You will also begin to realize that these great ideas also need to be put into production. In those terms, you need awareness of what the profession demands also.

Using the correct tools

It is important to use the appropriate software if you want to create detailed typographic design matter. At one time, having knowledge of software programs for setting typography wasn't much of a concern for the typographic designer. Detailed specifications were given by the designer to be set by a compositor or typesetter. Technology was often bespoke and exclusive to a 'closed' industry. The work was conducted by experts with precise skills and knowledge of their specialist areas.

However, thanks to the personal computer, graphic design and typography today requires the designer to know not only about the subject of design itself, but also about how design will be produced and reproduced once finalized.

Page layout and document construction software are best used for typographic work. They allow for precise typographic specification and multiple page documents to be created; for the assemblage of different kinds of 'linked' matter to be used together (font information, photos and illustrations); and for designers to have an object-orientated method of describing content in use.

Photo manipulation software may be useful for some aspects of display typography or type as image, but this is really best for image-making or editing. This kind of software uses pixels to render the image. It can cause issues with the clarity of small type for printed matter because of 'anti-aliasing'. Anti-aliasing creates a very subtle blur between the edges of objects in pixel-based programs. This actually works very well for most things, particularly for type on screen, but it doesn't work well for small type for print. There are also issues with resolution and with the reproduction of colour/tone if not handled correctly. Furthermore, certain files from this type of program will not be editable once saved.

Likewise, illustration software is very useful for producing one-off and unique pieces, such as logotypes, or where there is a strong display element to the work. This kind of software uses the outlines of objects as the main reference source for rendering the work. This is useful because saved files can often be 'scalable' without loss of quality. They are resolution independent.

'A sculptor does not see his hammer and chisel when he is carving, but only the stone in front of him.'
Eric Gill
An Essay on Typography (1936)

Typography can be handled successfully within such programs with care. Photo and illustration software should be treated as being best for that for which they are primarily intended. Finally, word-processing software should be avoided for designing typographic documents.

You can certainly combine and link files generated with different software packages. However, this needs learning and practice to produce work to a good standard. Get to know the tools. Then start to get to know the right tools for the job.

What follows is a discussion of some important features common to the leading design layout software programs. These attributes have existed for many years and are likely to continue for many more.

The information is intended as a guide to help you to think about developing your working practice in relation to software. It does not lay down a set of rules as such, but rather provides information that you may find helpful within the early stages of learning to work with and to apply your practice in terms of production.

Remember, it is the design that is most important; software and hardware are only tools that can be used as a means to craft that design.

Above

Shown above is student work that utilizes photo, illustration and a document design program to create the desired typographic result.

Desktop revolution

The digital desktop design revolution began in the mid-1980s. A combination of rapid successive inventions and introductions culminated in a release of traditionally bound working relationships and practices between designers, typesetters, pre-press technicians and printers.

Between the introduction of the Apple Macintosh in 1984, the Apple LaserWriter in 1985, the first desktop printer to contain Adobe PostScript technology, and Aldus PageMaker for the Mac in 1985, design experienced a new paradigm shift, one in which design possibilities appeared seemingly endless. For the first time, it seemed that designers could work intuitively with a sense of complete freedom, given these new fluid tools of production.

Below
How pages work
together may influence
your choice of software.

Opposite top
Shown here is a
modular grid created
in a master page.

Opposite bottom
The A Master here is
used as a template for
the document pages.

Single and multi-page designs

Selecting software to produce single-page designs, such as posters and broadsheets, will require you to take into consideration what kind of design it is that you intend to produce.

If your typographic work is to be precise and accurate, and is to use columns and grid systems including baseline grids, then it is very likely that you will need to use a design layout program. If the work is to appear more 'image-like', that is to say that it will mainly consist of display typography, then the options are more open as to which kind of software to employ (and this can include photo and illustration software). Type that requires outline manipulation for display or decorative purposes will need to be treated almost as illustration. Files can then be saved and included within design layout programs to include additional typography if needed.

Alternately, if there are only small amounts of type to add, this can be done within the vector illustration software. Adding small and detailed type to work created in photo-image based software should always be avoided for print. Save the image then bring this into a design layout application in order to include text.

In addition to the advice for single page layouts, multi-page work will require some further consideration. If the work is to be a book, for example, then the main option when deciding upon software is to use a design layout application. This allows for precise and detailed typographic treatment. Images and illustrations can also be placed or linked within this kind of application.

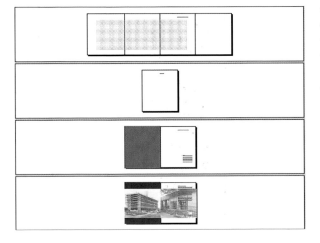

Master pages and guides

Master pages allow designers to specify particular attributes to any given page or group of pages within design layout programs. This is particularly useful for working with documents that will have multiple pages and grids, for example. Master pages are created as virtual templates for working pages within the program. Elements within these pages can then be edited and altered. Global changes can be made to pages already specified by using a particular master page.

A master page may contain any kind of element – text, pictures, rules, running heads and folios. Automatic page numbering is also a useful feature that master pages will facilitate. The latest versions of software now allow multi-page sizes to be created within a document and these can additionally be specified as master pages of differing sizes also. This is a useful and valuable new feature making 'artworking' for production a simpler task in some cases.

Many grids, columns and guides can be set up automatically by stating measurements and multiples of guides, rather than drawing each line individually within the program.

Remember: a grid should be used to aid design, not to force the design unnecessarily.

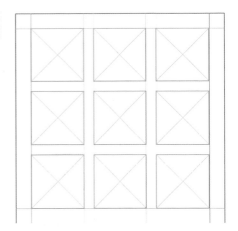

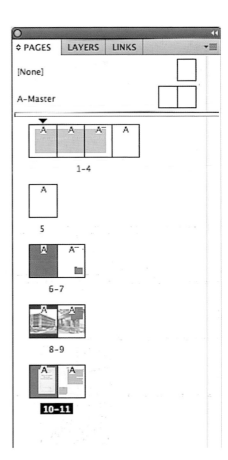

Type and style sheets

As was mentioned in chapter three, creating hierarchy within your typographic design may be an important factor to consider. Once you have worked out (and tested) which fonts to assign to your different levels of information structure, and you have tested these, it is a good idea to create styles within the design layout program that you are using.

Typographic styles can be created at the character level or paragraph level, allowing for information regarding font selection, type size, leading, colour, hyphenation and justification, alignment, indents, rules and so on to be assigned.

These can include numerous features and attributes already applied to the text. Once a style is saved, attributes can be changed within the style dialogue to apply changes globally for any given style. Text can then be highlighted and the required style applied.

Style sheets help to improve the accuracy and efficiency of your typographic specifications. Working with style sheets can also save hours of additional work when dealing with larger projects.

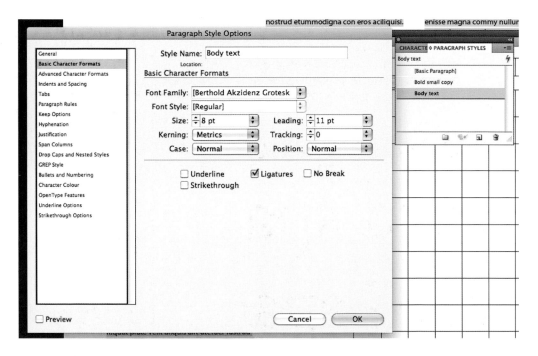

Type in original and output files

Typography produced within some programs may require the fonts to be converted to outlines in order to supply the artwork to printers or for production. Once this has been done, the type is no longer editable in the same manner as before. If you need to create outlines of your type make sure that you keep a copy of the file at the stage before this is done. You will then have a version that can be easily amended if needed. You may also need to create outlines of text where complicated foreign language settings or the use of special fonts may cause problems for the printer. It's important to keep separated editable versions of all of your work.

You should test your work as hard copies at various stages in the design process so that you can see what effect the changes will make to the artwork. Always check and supply hard copies of your final work when submitting your artwork for professional printing also.

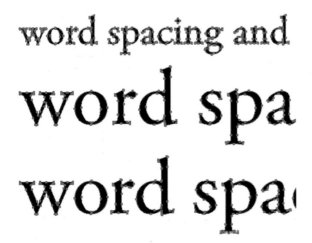

Opposite
Creating style sheets when working with type helps to increase accuracy and efficiency, thereby leaving more time for creative work.

Above
The student work shown here shows the complex setting of text as information design. It may be necessary to fix text depending on the type of output devices being used, in order to ensure that nothing moves or drops out.

Left
Outlining text means that it is no longer editable. Make sure that you always keep editable copies of work too!

Below
Crop marks and bleed
are necessary details of
production that should
not be overlooked.

Opposite
It can't be taken for
granted that what
you print as a proof
will be the same as
the final high-quality
finished work in term
of production. Get to
know how your printer(s)
behave and so what to
expect of them.

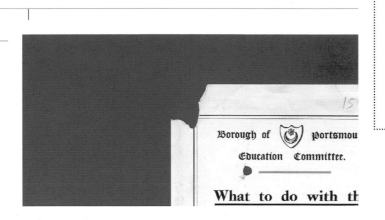

Portable document files

Portable document files such as PDFs (Portable Document Format) allow you to share your work across platforms for viewing and for output. This is sometimes a necessary way to supply your finished work for high quality printing within the design industry. This kind of file is usually 'exported' from the original software program; however, some programs allow for these as a 'save as' feature, enabling them to be read back into the program as editable files.

In terms of how fonts are handled by PDFs, it is not necessary to outline these first, as font information can be embedded within the PDF depending upon the settings used.

This is useful because it means that the recipient of the file does not need to have the same font that you used when creating the work in order to view or print this. As before, if the work is ready for final output, you need to firstly make sure that image size (dpi), colour space, bleed and crop marks are included as necessary depending on the nature of the work. The UK Pass4Press website offers very useful guides for setting up accepted PDF industry standard files. See <www.ppa.co.uk> for more information.

'For me, typography is a triangular relationship between design idea, typographic elements and printing technique.'
Wolfgang Weingart

Proofing

When we work on the computer, we tend to see what it is on screen as being correct. We may even print to our desktop printer and be fairly happy with the result. However, when you are producing typographic design work for high-quality printing, much of the small detail needs to be checked and tested in terms of assessing if this will withstand output at high resolution. Images, colours, fonts, format, bleed and crop marks all need to be checked and tested also. Colour separations may also need to be printed and checked to ensure that files will behave as expected. One of the most common problems that will be seen are differences in 'typographic colour' and the 'weight' of text type between printing from a desktop printer and high quality litho.

The desktop printer can only give a proof of your work and unfortunately in most cases this is not accurate to that which will be seen as the final litho print. Test printers with different resolution outputs. Also test the difference between laser and inkjet technology for your proofs. If testing text type, it may be necessary to use a printer with black-only toner that outputs at 2400dpi or above to get an accurate sense of how your text will behave in final print production. Also, some desktop printers have software that interpolates font data to give the best possible view of your typography; however, this may not be the same as how the data is finally interpreted when in production. These are all minute details but they are also worth bearing in mind. Always remember, the job's not over 'til it's over!

Conclusion

This book has set out to outline some of the key points that you may need to consider as you begin to work with type. It also aims to get you to think about what you may need to consider for the future when developing your typographic awareness.

Like many subjects, most of your learning will come from experience and practice. However, some of the aspects of typographic practice highlighted in this book are those that you can engage with readily.

Typography takes time to master. Even then, there are always things to learn or improve upon. In a way, this is what makes the subject fascinating – and somewhat obsessive at times – for those who devote themselves to it. It is also an extremely important subject with great depth.

Typography gives 'voice' or 'accent' to a text; it is the way in which a text is 'delivered'. It is therefore through typography that we make tangible the visual communication of language. Even in the simple act of choosing a font, we potentially alter the way in which the reader will perceive any given typographically set text.

For someone involved in designing communications, the use of typography represents an important consideration. Whilst the content is ultimately most important, the care given to typography should not be neglected nor underestimated as a tool for communication in itself.

This book has concentrated mainly on elementary practical aspects of the subject of typography. There is a wealth of knowledge relating history, practice and technology to draw upon that has not been covered. In reality, no single book can cover all of this.

If you have carefully read through the chapters, digested what has been described and are beginning to apply some of this to your practice, then hopefully you are setting out on what will be an enjoyable typographic journey that may have many twists and turns along the way, but one that will keep you happily occupied and even entertained for many years to come!

IJK

ln

opq

IJV

Bibliography

Useful further reading

Baines P. & Haslam A. (2002) *Type and Typography*. London: Laurence King

Baudin F. (1989) *How Typography Works (and why it is still important)*. London: Lund Humphries

Binns B. (1989) *Better Type*. New York: Watson-Guptill Publications

Bringhurst R. (2004) *The Elements of Typographic Style*. Point Roberts: Hartley & Marks

Friedl F. (1998) *Typography: When, Who, How*. Konemann UK Ltd

Grey N. & Nash R. (1976) *Nineteenth Century Ornamented Typefaces*. New edn. London: Faber & Faber

Hochuli J. (2008) *Detail in Typography*. London: Hyphen Press

Hochuli J. & Kinross R. (2003) *Designing Books: Practice and Theory*. London: Hyphen Press

Jardi E. (2007) *Twenty-two Tips on Typography*. New York: Actar

Jaspert W.P., Berry W.T. & Johnson A.F. (1983) *Encyclopaedia of Typefaces*, rev. edn. London: Blandford

Johnson A.F. (1966) *Type Designs*, 3rd revised edn. London: Andre Deutsch

Kinross R. (2008) *Modern Typography: An essay in critical history*. London: Hyphen Press

Lupton E. (2010) *Thinking with Type*. Princeton Architectural Press

McLean R. (1980) *Thames & Hudson Manual of Typography*. London: Thames & Hudson

Müller-Brockmann J. (2009) *Grid Systems in Graphic Design*. Sulgen: Verlag Niggli

Rafaeli A. (2006) *Book Typography*. Delaware: Oak Knoll Press & London: The British Library

Ruder E. (2001) *Typographie*, 7th edn. Sulgen: Verlag Niggli

Spencer H. (1990) *Pioneers of Modern Typography*, 2nd edn revised. London: Lund Humphries

Spiekermann E. & Ginger E. M.
(2002) *Stop Stealing Sheep and Find Out How Type Works.* California: Adobe Press

Steer V. (c.1935) *Printing Design and Layout: The Manual for Printers, Typographers and all Designers and Users of Printing and Advertising.* London: Virtue

Steinberg S.H. (1961) *Five Hundred Years of Printing,* 2nd edn. Middlesex: Penguin

Sutton J. & Bartram A. (1988) *An Atlas of Typeforms.* Ware: Wordsworth Editions

Tracy W. (1986) *Letters of Credit: A View of Type Design.* London: Gordon Fraser

Tschichold J. (1996) *The Form of the Book: Essays on the Morality of Good Design.* Point Roberts: Hartley & Marks

Tschichold J. (2006) *The New Typography.* California: University of California Press

Tschichold J. (1992) *Treasury of Alphabets and Lettering.* London: Lund Humphries

Updike D.B. (1937) *Printing Types, Their History, Forms and Use – A Study in Survivals,* 2nd edn. London: Oxford University Press

Vanderlands R. Licko Z. & Gray M.E. (1993) *Emigre: Graphic Design into the Digital Realm,* 2nd edn. London: Oxford University Press

alignment

The positioning of text within the page margins. Alignment can be ranged left, ranged right, justified, or centered.

ascender

The part of lower case letters that protrudes above the x-height.

baseline

The invisible line on which the characters in a typeface sit.

body text

Sometimes referred to as 'body-copy'. This is the continuous reading matter usually set at small sizes such as 10, 11 and 12pt.

bullet

A dot or other special character placed at the left of items in a list to show that they are individual, but related, points.

cap height

The height from the baseline to the top of the upper case letters.

descender

The part of a lower case letter that descends below the baseline.

display font

A font that has been designed to work at large point sizes. These can often have decorative qualities or details that at small point sizes may not render well.

dpi

Dots per inch. Used to indicate the quality of resolution. As a general rule: 300dpi for print and 72dpi (96 in some cases) for screen.

drop cap

The first capital letter of a paragraph when set in a larger point size and aligned with the top of the first line and occupies a number of lines of type in depth. A three-line drop cap is often considered to work well.

ellipsis

A punctuation mark consisting of three dots in a row. Used to indicate omissions. Sometimes referred to as a three-dot leader.

em dash

The em dash is used to indicate a break in a sentence, particularly in book work. This is usually not used with word spaces either side.

em, em space, em quad

A unit of relational measurement. Traditionally, the em is defined as the body width of the upper case M in any given typeface and point size. It can be thought of simply as the current point size in use. E.g. in 12-point type, em is 12 points.

en, en space, en quad

A unit of relational measurement. The en is defined as the body width of the upper case N. It is regarded as half the width of an em.

en dash

The en dash can be used to indicate a range of values or a break in a sentence. When used with numerals, a word space either side of the en dash should not be used, although some slight adjustment of space may be required. When used in text, this should be set with a word space either side.

font

A font is sometimes referred to as a collection of characters of one typeface design.

font family

A font family is sometimes referred to as a collection of characters of one typeface design and its related variants, i.e. roman, bold, italic, etc.

glyph

Glyph is used to indicate a single character within a font. This can be a letterform, punctuation, numeral or symbol, etc.

hanging indent

The first line of a paragraph when aligned with the left margin, and the remaining lines are all indented an equal amount. This is sometimes referred to as an out-dent.

italic

A slanting or script-like variant of a typeface. Upright variants are usually referred to as roman.

justified

A style applied, where text is forced to align on both the left and right margins. This can often be found in the book-setting for novels, etc. It can sometimes cause problems with word spacing if not adjusted correctly.

kerning

Adjustment of horizontal space between individual characters in typographic setting.

leading

Inter-linear spacing. Traditionally strips of lead set between lines of metal type used to adjust line spacing. In digital type, the leading can be thought of as the measurement or distance between baselines in typographic setting.

letter spacing

The space between letters. Sometimes when adjusted, this is referred to as tracking.

ligature

Two or more letters joined together that create a single character. For example: fi, fl, ffi, ffl, etc.

These are often used for aesthetic purposes only. Joined characters used to indicate unique sounds such as: Æ æ, etc. are referred to as dipthongs.

margin

The space around the text-image area on a page.

oblique

A slanting version of a typeface – not the same as italic.

OpenType

A font format that allows for larger character sets with enhanced user capabilities.

paragraph rules

Typographic rules usually set above and/or below the paragraph.

pica

A unit of typographic measurement equal to 12pt. Approximately 4.24mm or 1/6 of an inch.

point

A unit of typographic measurement. There are approximately 72 points to the inch.

point size

The measurement usually given for type. This is often the height of the 'body' upon which the letter sits.

raised cap

Where the first capital letter of a paragraph is set to a larger point size. This is aligned on the baseline of the first line of text.

ranged left

Text that is aligned on the left-hand side. This is sometimes referred to as ragged right.

ranged right

Text that is aligned on the right-hand side. This is sometimes referred to as ragged left.

reverse-out

A technique where text, etc. is made to 'knock-out' from an area of solid colour so that the text appears as the colour of the paper, etc. and the ink surrounds.

roman

The upright version of a typeface.

sans serif

A typeface without serifs.

serif

Small strokes included at the terminals of the main strokes of a letter.

set solid

Type set without additional leading. E.g. 24/24pt indicates 24pt type on 24pt leading.

style

Appearance, such as italic and bold, that make up the variants of a type family.

symbol

Usually referred to as non-alphanumeric characters.

tracking

The between characters in a block of text when considered overall. Sometimes also referred to as letter spacing.

typeface

Letters, numbers, and symbols that make up a type design. A typeface can often be part of a larger family of fonts. Traditionally in metal type, the typeface was literally the design on the face of the type used as the surface to print from.

typeface family

A collection of typefaces designed to work together and usually sharing common attributes across related variants.

typographic colour

This is referred to the evenness or apparent greyness which a body of text is perceived has having. Leading, letter spacing and word spacing can be adjusted to alter this quality in set text of a given typeface.

unjustified

Text that is not justified.

weight

The relative boldness or darkness of characters considered as variants of a typeface design. For example: light, bold, extra-bold, and black.

white space

An important consideration in the layout of typographic and graphic design matter. White space refers to areas of a layout where text and image matter are purposefully not employed. This helps create structure, balance, and visual rest or punctuation in a composition.

width

One of the possible variations of a typeface design. Condensed and expanded are examples of width variants.

word spacing

The average space between words. This is often the approximate width of the lower case 'i'.

x-height

Traditionally the height of the lower case letter x. It can also be referred to as the height of the body of lower case letters in a font, excluding the ascenders and descenders. X-heights may vary greatly in different typefaces yet still having the same point size.

Index

Page numbers in *italics*
denote illustrations.

Acknowledgements and credits

This book is dedicated to my wife Lynne and daughter Georgie.

I would like to thank all those that have allowed their work to be shown in this book.

Thanks also to the following former students whose examples of work have been shown: Charlotte Eason (p.17); Tim Hampson (p.109); Zhi Long Huang (p.159); Poppy Hurst (pp.50–51); and Jodie Silsby (p.163).

A special thank you to Daniel Alexander for his photography of artefacts and of a printing workshop.

I must also thank my editor Colette Meacher for her support, understanding and patience.

Particular thanks to:

Ben Parker, MadeThought
Catherine Dixon
Gerard Unger
Hamish Muir, 8vo
Henrik Kubel, A2 Graphics
Huang Zilhong
Ian Cartlidge, Cartlidge Levene Ltd.
Jeremy Tankard, Jeremy Tankard Photography
Nick Bell, Nick Bell Design
Paulus M. Dreibholz, Atelier for Typography and Graphic Design
Phil Baines
Why Not Associates

Photograph on p.15 by Marcus Ginns
Photograph on p.115 by Sue O'Brien

BASICS
TYPOGRAPHY

Working with ethics

Lynne Elvins
Naomi Goulder

Publisher's note

The subject of ethics is not new, yet its consideration within the applied visual arts is perhaps not as prevalent as it might be. Our aim here is to help a new generation of students, educators and practitioners find a methodology for structuring their thoughts and reflections in this vital area.

AVA Publishing hopes that these **Working with ethics** pages provide a platform for consideration and a flexible method for incorporating ethical concerns in the work of educators, students and professionals. Our approach consists of four parts:

The **introduction** is intended to be an accessible snapshot of the ethical landscape, both in terms of historical development and current dominant themes.

The **framework** positions ethical consideration into four areas and poses questions about the practical implications that might occur. Marking your response to each of these questions on the scale shown will allow your reactions to be further explored by comparison.

The **case study** sets out a real project and then poses some ethical questions for further consideration. This is a focus point for a debate rather than a critical analysis so there are no predetermined right or wrong answers.

A selection of **further reading** for you to consider areas of particular interest in more detail.

Ethical: awareness/ reflection/ debate

Ethics is a complex subject that interlaces the idea of responsibilities to society with a wide range of considerations relevant to the character and happiness of the individual. It concerns virtues of compassion, loyalty and strength, but also of confidence, imagination, humour and optimism. As introduced in ancient Greek philosophy, the fundamental ethical question is: *what should I do?* How we might pursue a 'good' life not only raises moral concerns about the effects of our actions on others, but also personal concerns about our own integrity.

In modern times the most important and controversial questions in ethics have been the moral ones. With growing populations and improvements in mobility and communications, it is not surprising that considerations about how to structure our lives together on the planet should come to the forefront. For visual artists and communicators, it should be no surprise that these considerations will enter into the creative process.

Some ethical considerations are already enshrined in government laws and regulations or in professional codes of conduct. For example, plagiarism and breaches of confidentiality can be punishable offences. Legislation in various nations makes it unlawful to exclude people with disabilities from accessing information or spaces. The trade of ivory as a material has been banned in many countries. In these cases, a clear line has been drawn under what is unacceptable.

But most ethical matters remain open to debate, among experts and lay-people alike, and in the end we have to make our own choices on the basis of our own guiding principles or values.

Is it more ethical to work for a charity than for a commercial company? Is it unethical to create something that others find ugly or offensive?

Specific questions such as these may lead to other questions that are more abstract. For example, is it only effects on humans (and what they care about) that are important, or might effects on the natural world require attention too?

Is promoting ethical consequences justified even when it requires ethical sacrifices along the way? Must there be a single unifying theory of ethics (such as the Utilitarian thesis that the right course of action is always the one that leads to the greatest happiness of the greatest number), or might there always be many different ethical values that pull a person in various directions?

As we enter into ethical debate and engage with these dilemmas on a personal and professional level, we may change our views or change our view of others. The real test though is whether, as we reflect on these matters, we change the way we act as well as the way we think. Socrates, the 'father' of philosophy, proposed that people will naturally do 'good' if they know what is right. But this point might only lead us to yet another question: *how do we know what is right?*

You
What are your ethical beliefs?

Central to everything you do will be your attitude to people and issues around you. For some people, their ethics are an active part of the decisions they make every day as a consumer, a voter or a working professional. Others may think about ethics very little and yet this does not automatically make them unethical. Personal beliefs, lifestyle, politics, nationality, religion, gender, class or education can all influence your ethical viewpoint.

Using the scale, where would you place yourself? What do you take into account to make your decision? Compare results with your friends or colleagues.

Your client
What are your terms?

Working relationships are central to whether ethics can be embedded into a project, and your conduct on a day-to-day basis is a demonstration of your professional ethics. The decision with the biggest impact is whom you choose to work with in the first place. Cigarette companies or arms traders are often-cited examples when talking about where a line might be drawn, but rarely are real situations so extreme. At what point might you turn down a project on ethical grounds and how much does the reality of having to earn a living affect your ability to choose?

Using the scale, where would you place a project? How does this compare to your personal ethical level?

01 02 03 04 05 06 07 08 09 10

01 02 03 04 05 06 07 08 09 10

Your specifications
What are the impacts of your materials?

In relatively recent times, we are learning that many natural materials are in short supply. At the same time, we are increasingly aware that some man-made materials can have harmful, long-term effects on people or the planet. How much do you know about the materials that you use? Do you know where they come from, how far they travel and under what conditions they are obtained? When your creation is no longer needed, will it be easy and safe to recycle? Will it disappear without a trace? Are these considerations your responsibility or are they out of your hands?

Using the scale, mark how ethical your material choices are.

Your creation
What is the purpose of your work?

Between you, your colleagues and an agreed brief, what will your creation achieve? What purpose will it have in society and will it make a positive contribution? Should your work result in more than commercial success or industry awards? Might your creation help save lives, educate, protect or inspire? Form and function are two established aspects of judging a creation, but there is little consensus on the obligations of visual artists and communicators toward society, or the role they might have in solving social or environmental problems. If you want recognition for being the creator, how responsible are you for what you create and where might that responsibility end?

Using the scale, mark how ethical the purpose of your work is.

01 02 03 04 05 06 07 08 09 10

01 02 03 04 05 06 07 08 09 10

An aspect of typography that may raise ethical issues is its capacity to make information accessible or understandable to the reader. Creative use of typography can emphasise meaning and embed emotion in words. In this way, typography can facilitate verbal and visual communication, and in turn give rise to fundamental questions about the role of a given piece of text.

Will the text instruct, inform or helpfully guide the receiver towards beneficial information of some kind? Or might it confuse, frighten or alienate all but a select few? Does a typographer have a responsibility to always be as clear, informative and legible as possible? Or are there occasions where the decorative treatment of script is far more important than the ability to read the words? How much responsibility should the typographer assume for the message, as well as for the means by which it is delivered?

Graffiti has been found around the world and throughout history, from the catacombs of Rome to the Mayan temple walls of Tikal in Mesoamerica. Graffiti found in Pompeii, with its messages of political rhetoric or Latin curses, provides us with insights into the daily lives of people during the first century. Graffiti continues to tell us about life today, as well as directly reflecting the writer's views of society.

In France during the student protests and general strike of May 1968, revolutionary anarchist and situationist slogans covered the walls of Paris, articulating the spirit of the age. In the US, around the same time, street gangs were using graffiti as a means to mark territory. Signatures or 'tags', rather than slogans, were used by writers such as TOPCAT 126 and COOL EARL. CORNBREAD, credited by some as the father of modern graffiti, began his career by writing 'Cornbread loves Cynthia' all over his school. In the early 1970s, graffiti moved to New York and writers such as TAKI 183 began to add their street number to their nickname. Tags began to take on a calligraphic appearance in order to stand out, and also began to grow in size and include thick outlines. Bubble lettering was initially popular before 'wildstyle' – a complicated creation of interlocking letters using lots of arrows and connections – came to define the art of graffiti.

The use of graffiti as a portrayal of rebellious urban style made it attractive to creatives operating within mainstream culture. In 2001, fashion designer and artist Stephen Sprouse, in collaboration with fellow designer Marc Jacobs, designed a limited-edition line of Louis Vuitton bags that featured graffiti scrawled over the company's monogrammed pattern.

Despite the fact that graffiti has now become both a familiar and accepted artistic form within everyday society, it remains controversial. There is a clear distinction between graffiti employed typographically by a designer or artist, to graffiti that is applied to either public or private property. In most countries, defacing property without permission is deemed to be vandalism and is therefore punishable by law. Governments spend vast sums of public money removing graffiti. A 1995 study by the National Graffiti Information Network estimated that the cost of cleaning up graffiti in the US amounted annually to approximately USD$8 billion.

If it is illegal, is it also unethical to graffiti on someone else's property?

Are companies exploiting graffiti if they use it to sell commercial goods?

Would you be prepared to be imprisoned to communicate a message?

A word is not a crystal, transparent and unchanged; it is the skin of a living thought, and may vary greatly in color and content according to the circumstances and the time in which it is used.

Oliver Wendell Holmes Jr

AIGA
Design Business and Ethics
2007, AIGA

Eaton, M.M.
Aesthetics and the Good Life
1989, Associated University Press

Ellison, D.
Ethics and Aesthetics in European Modernist Literature:
From the Sublime to the Uncanny
2001, Cambridge University Press

Fenner, D.E.W. (Ed)
Ethics and the Arts:
An Anthology
1995, Garland Reference Library of Social Science

Gini, A. and M., Alexei M.
Case Studies in Business Ethics
2005, Prentice Hall

McDonough, W. and Braungart, M.
Cradle to Cradle:
Remaking the Way We Make Things
2002, North Point Press

Papanek, V.
Design for the Real World:
Making to Measure
1972, Thames & Hudson

United Nations Global Compact
The Ten Principles
www.unglobalcompact.org/AboutTheGC/TheTenPrinciples/index.html